Praise for Erle Dardick's
Get Catering and Grow Sales!

A Strategic Perspective for the Multi-Unit Restaurant Executive

"Erle brings to the table a unique combination of day to day operator experience and technology know how. In *Get Catering and Grow Sales!* Erle has captured the importance of looking at catering from a strategic perspective, taking into account the brand building that occurs through the natural cross-pollination of restaurant and catering sales. With his strong operator background Erle clearly understands the value that a thoughtful strategic plan will bring to any company considering catering... *Get Catering and Grow Sales!* is a must read for any executive considering catering as a way to grow revenues and brand awareness!" - **Dave Wolfgram, Chief Executive Officer for Forklift Brands (Boudin Bakeries)**

"This book should be required reading for every restaurant executive before they attempt to create a catering strategy. Erle understands that catering not only builds sales, but when executed properly develops brand loyalty and brand equity, adding value to the experience of our brands. Erle's insights can form the foundation of a strategic and profitable catering business. As well, he emphasizes the importance of catering to help deliver the message of our brands to our guests. Erle is passionate about the power of creating positive brand goodwill through business catering and this philosophy of brand protection is cornerstone to all his ideas." - **Annica Kreider, Vice President of Marketing for McAlister's Deli**

"As with his catering operation, Erle serves up a tasty offering in *Get Catering and Grow Sales!* where you, the reader, focus on the quality of the product and not all the work that it took to deliver it. His blueprint for success is at the same time both universal and concept-specific. Every brand is different and provides its guests with a unique offering. But, as Erle makes clear, every brand faces the same operational issues when it comes to successful catering. As a marketer, I want to ensure that our guests experience our brand the same way at every touch point: in the café, on the phone, or in the boardroom. In *Get Catering and Grow Sales!* Erle explains what is required behind the scenes to make that happen with catering. If we are going to be able to focus on our guests, we need the shared strategy and systems in place that Erle describes in his book." - **Ed Frechette, Senior Vice President of Marketing for Au Bon Pain**

"Over the past 15 years Erle has demonstrated his visionary capability in the multi-unit restaurant environment. His book clearly outlines one of the next big top line opportunities for multi-unit restaurant operators worldwide. Driving catering sales volume at the unit level creates economic benefit for everyone in the supply chain - *Get Catering and Grow Sales!*" - **Frank Geier, President of Gordon Food Services**

"Right up front Erle states that the ideas presented in *Get Catering and Grow Sales!* are not his alone. Well, that's debatable; but overall Erle clearly lays out the blueprint from his many years of personal experience and firsthand knowledge towards the path to new catering sales growth. Erle hits a home run explaining that it's all about strategy first, passion second, energy third and finally the execution necessary to round all the bases. Catering is the new path to double-digit sales and profit growth. For any executive in the restaurant industry this is a must read. I highly recommend it!" - **Dan Dominguez, Chief Operating Officer for Einstein Noah Restaurant Group, Inc.**

"When I am asked by multi-unit restaurant operators what they can do to increase sales, I always tell them to focus on developing their catering business. No other single decision can have as huge an impact on both the top and bottom lines during even the worst economic times. In *Get Catering and Grow Sales!* Erle explains how you can you can get your share of this huge market. I have known him for years, and his ideas really work." – **George Green, Vice President of Bread & Company**

"Erle has captured the how, what and why of multi-unit restaurant catering execution done right. His passion for the segment and understanding of why there is a right way to cater is invaluable to the multi-unit restaurant operator. *Get Catering and Grow Sales!* should be required reading for concept heads, multi-unit restaurant managers, store level managers and the sales person in the field. Now there is no excuse to leave these sales dollars on the table. He has given our industry the path to successful catering execution." - **Jeff Drake, President of Go Roma Italian Kitchen**

"Erle's recommendation that traditional multi-unit restaurant operators consider expanding into off-premise services is both logical and compelling. Having gained considerable experience as an entrepreneur and deli operator before branching into MonkeyMedia Software, Erle has become an expert in the day-to-day complexities of the modern multi-unit restaurant environment. He therefore approaches both the challenges and the opportunities with a singular perspective with his eyes wide open. Erle also understands that success in any off-site endeavor hinges on the operator's ability to translate his or her unique brand equity and attributes of core menu offerings in novel and appealing ways. Whether or not you decide his approach is for you, you'll be struck by the combination of his creativity and entrepreneurial insight that he brings to the table." - **Marc Halperin, Chief Operating Officer for the Center for Culinary Development**

"Erle presents emphatic catering truths in *Get Catering and Grow Sales!* Listen, learn and LIVE these truths to develop your catering revenue stream and watch it grow. He methodically presents everything you need to know to enable doing it right and doing it right now. The realities of aligning organizational resources and internal execution around catering revenue potential are well presented, real, and most complete. Erle and the team at MonkeyMedia Software have been knowledgeable and helpful contributors to "connecting the many dots" expressed so comprehensively in *Get Catering and Grow Sales!*" - **Wayne Alexander, Catering Director, Einstein Noah Restaurant Group, Inc.**

"With all of the choices for business catering, progressive brands from pizza to delis to bakery cafés, should embrace this strategy, fund the additional start-up costs and go sell it. Erle provides a compass for all multi-unit restaurant operators including the Pizza segment. Catering is a huge opportunity for all of us! I highly recommend his strategies and encourage each of you to follow his thought leadership on this very important subject."- **Ed Zimmerman, President, The Food Connector**

"Any restaurateur with multiple units that's thinking of getting into catering would do well to read Erle's book. As he says many times, Erle's learned a lot from his mistakes and put that learning to good use to do effective catering—no reason the rest of us shouldn't get to learn from his experiences. It's safe to say that anyone that puts Erle's teaching into effect will save time, money and stress, and increase catering sales in the process"– **Ari Weinzweig, Co-Founder of Zingerman's Delicatessen**

100% of the net proceeds from the sale of this book are being donated* to

Share Our Strength's goal is to end childhood hunger in America. Working with others, we believe we can do this by 2015.

It's not enough to make sure America's children have *enough* to eat; we must make sure they are getting the *nutrition* they need to live healthy, active lives.

That is why **Share Our Strength's highest priority is to make sure that every child in America gets the nutritious food he or she needs to learn, grow and thrive.** We are doing this by improving the access families all across the country have to healthy, affordable food and by working at the state and city level. Our "No Kid Hungry" strategy has four key components that, together, provide children with the nutritious food they need where they live, learn and play, by:

- Creating public-private **partnerships** at the state and city level to map out comprehensive, measurable plans to end child hunger in those areas.
- **Building public awareness** about the problem of childhood hunger and solutions to end it.
- Investing in communities with **grants** to organizations whose work improves access to nutritious foods or that educate families about such programs.
- **Educating children and families** about nutritious, affordable food.

*ending December 2012.

What I cherish most of all

My wife, Karin, and my three beautiful children –
Jonah, Gabriel and Maya. You make it all worthwhile.

"Almost all quality improvement comes via simplification of design, manufacturing... layout, processes, and procedures."

- Tom Peters, author of *In Search of Excellence*

Get Catering and Grow Sales!

A Strategic Perspective for The Multi-Unit Restaurant Executive

with a special introduction by Tom Feltenstein, CEO & Founder of Power Marketing Academy

Erle Dardick MBA
CEO MonkeyMedia Software

CONTENTS

Why Dumb Guys Make So Much Money xvii

Foreword xxiii

Some things we believe in at MonkeyMedia Software.................... xxvi

Preface.. xxvii

Sitting in a quiet catering space...................................... xxxi

I just couldn't sit here and watch anymore! So, I wrote instead! xxxi

Credit where credit is due... xxxiii

Catering in the years ahead xxxv

PART I – The Story 1

Tony's Deli (1996), where my foodservice venture began........................ 3

How we put the "software" in MonkeyMedia............................... 7

How MonkeyMedia Software became an industry leader. 8

We will lead the way for the world's multi-unit restaurant
brands – big and small... 11

All brands, big and small, operate in challenging times....................... 13

A hamburger is a sandwich! Sandwiches are great for catering! 17

Make catering part of your core business!................................ 18

Catering is a serious business! 19

Taking catering seriously 21

Rapid sales increase with few incremental costs 23

How do we implement the "business of catering"
into our operations? 24

Dignity and professionalism will create a solid return on
investment 26

Adding catering services will help our brands build more local
community 30

PART II: THE THEORY – One Monkey's Perspective 33

Let's look at the academics 35

First we need executive alignment followed by a thoughtful menu 35

Driving incremental sales is the ONLY reason to do catering 37

A visual table to help with the math 39

Leveraging our brands 41

Pulling our teams together 44

There is a big opportunity for those that want to seize it! 45

Growing catering sales will create wealth for our community 47

Leveraging assets is simply smart business. But we still need to invest! .. 49

Catering just makes sense at the unit level. 52

Our unique complexity as multi-unit restaurant operators 54

Franchising adds even more complexity and dynamics 54

Technology options – our community is overwhelmed! 56

Catering is basic business 57

What's happening with catering in our multi-unit restaurant
community? 58

PART III: Let's go deeper into
Get Catering and Grow Sales! 59

Retail dollar out of manufacturing rents 61

Document your strategy 64

Create an enforceable policy-and-procedure manual for catering............65

Develop marketing materials that are catering specific.........66

Hire the right catering sales staff 70

Extending catering to the franchised and licensed communities............70

Growing catering is a GREAT business decision!...................73

Some core functional areas of a multi-unit catering operation...............73

How to get catering sales...................74

The psychology of the catering sale....................74

The sales methodology for growing more catering revenue 77

What are you actually selling? 80

Growing catering revenue requires business-to-business selling 80

Relationship selling needs to be part of your core strategy 81

Let's discuss menus for growing catering sales.......................82

Order execution is the key to growing catering sales!...........83

Creating a reliable, predictable and scalable catering experience............86

Pharmaceutical reps – A special relationship.........................86

The promo package: Sampling sells catering!....................87

Cold calling to build catering sales 88

Traditional advertising – how to use it to grow catering sales 89

Walk-in catering sales – how do you handle the customer? 89

Telephone work – be relentless and watch catering sales soar! 90

Referrals are the most powerful tool you have for growing
catering sales 91

Mobilizing your most important resources – your frontline people.........92

Get business cards – lots of them! 93

Recognizing the different characteristics of a potential
catering order 93

Group orders – the lunchroom table 94

Group orders – the boardroom table 94

Group orders – training seminars and tours 95

Great customer service will grow catering sales!.....................................95

Who are your clients and what do they look like? 99

Relationships are very important in this catering business 99

Logging problems so that you can make it right! 100

Order entry is the frontline when it comes to catering. 101

Order follow-up will increase catering sales and further strengthen
your customer relationships. 102

Asking for more business will get you more business!...........................103

Production efficiency will grow your sales!..104

Internal planning – for tomorrow's catering orders..............................105

Menu development will shift consumer behavior and drive
more sales!..107

The right packaging is critical to growing sales! 108

Trays and platters – the cornerstone of a solid catering business 110

Box lunches – Focus on volume 111

Beverages – Think about creating a proprietary beverage 111

Hot food vs. cold food...112

Manufacturing efficiency will help to grow sales! 113

Planning the catering production process properly will create more

capacity for growing sales! 116

Production time is really "assembly time"! 116

Solid vendor management can grow sales!..117

Using your existing labor more effectively will increase your overall

unit level margins!...117

You will live or die by your order execution!..119

Preparing for distribution properly will be critical to your

customers' experience! 121

Distribution methodologies are a strategic and managerial

preference 121

Should you manage drivers internally or contract third-party drivers?

The big debate! 122

Saying "please" and "thank you" at the delivery point can help grow

catering sales! 123

Some key responsibilities for your primary drivers 123

A few thoughts regarding outsourcing drivers 123

Catering finance and accounting is customer service work and will

have a positive impact on growing sales!.. 124

Accounts Receivables... 124

The right billing system will help grow sales!................................... 125

Why using existing POS assets for catering transactions is dangerous

for your brand.. 126

Pricing strategy 128

Management and metrics.. 128

Some additional metrics to consider tracking. 129

How to make a profit with catering 130

The right technology and software will grow sales!........................... 133

Committing to the right catering software system. 133

Is POS integration required for catering sales? 134

Conclusion – what's the right strategy for your organization? 136

Appendix: Get Catering and Grow Sales!: A Discussion Series 138

Acknowledgements... 139

My sincere gratitude 140

Why Dumb Guys Make So Much Money

by Tom Feltenstein

Funny thing about genius. It almost always shows up dressed like an idiot. Take Albert Einstein, for example. How do you trust a guy with a haircut like that? If he were your neighbor you wouldn't lend him a hammer for fear he'd break the thing. Did you know he couldn't even tie his own shoes? Go figure.

And how come the smartest guy in the room almost always turns out to be the last one you should take advice from? Get past the suit and the power tie and there's usually nobody home.

Give me the dumb guy every time. He's got a way of sticking with a problem. Making things happen. And making money. Lots of it. I've watched dumb guys in companies large and small make zillions of dollars, time and time again.

How does that happen? I wondered.

I've been lucky enough in my career to work with some of the dumbest guys around. Guys like President Ronald Regan, Ed Rensi – Current CEO of Tom and Eddies and former CEO of McDonald's, Fred DeLuca - Subway cofounder, Jon Luther – chairman of Dunkin' Donuts and Ray Kroc – the founder and visionary behind McDonald's. And now this guy - Erle Dardick. Another dumb guy. What the heck do all these dumb guys know that I don't?

Get Catering and Grow Sales! answers that question.

Erle came up with the answer by working with some of the dumbest guys in the world. Guys who didn't go to Harvard, or Stanford, or polish their skills at a top-rated business school. Guys who simply went about the business of doing what dumb guys do. Doing what works. Doing things that are blindingly obvious, once you understand them. Doing stuff that touches ordinary people in extraordinary ways. Once you see it, once it's explained to you as Erle does very simply and straightforwardly in this book, over and over and over again like a sledgehammer, *whack, whack, whack,* you suddenly get the message, which is: Dumb stuff works. Dumb stuff works. Dumb stuff works. And dumb stuff, you will learn, is really, really, really smart to do.

Like catering.

Now for the first time in our industry, this book presents one monkey's perspectives on a system that can make a whole lot of money for you, no matter what kind of restaurants you're running, provided you're dumb enough to give it a shot. I can't believe Erle's dumb enough to share this stuff with you, but apparently he is.

A very smart guy once asked me how I would go about growing my business if I really set my mind to it. The answer I gave him prompted a reply that all smart guys would give. I said, simply, that if I really, really wanted to grow my business – grow it a LOT --- I would put 1,000 energized straight commission evangelists on the streets of North America. And give them a simple story to tell. And the business would explode with growth.

The guy looked at me like I was a moron.

"Straight commission sales people?" he asked. "What about marketing, what about media, what about the *Internet?*"

The guy was very, very smart. He knew that straight-commission sales people are a thing of the past. Like tired old brush salesmen tramping door to door with their beat-up suitcases and their shiny suits. He knew that marketing, media, and the Internet are about *exposure*. And he knew that exposure was expensive, that marketing costs money. Serious money. And it's sophisticated. Seriously sophisticated. And because of that, it calls for expensive, sophisticated people to do it. He knew all that, and as a result, he just *knew* that if it didn't cost a lot of money, and if it didn't require a lot of really, really smart people to do it, it couldn't be very interesting and it would never be successful. Successful ideas need big budgets to make them work. Armies of smart people. Slick commercials and animated spinning logos on interactive websites and massive media plans. Serious money. My plan was just, well, dumb. After all, if all I had going for me was 1,000 sales people on straight commission, my business couldn't be a very sexy business, now could it? And sexy is what marketing's all about. Sexy is marketing's middle name. Sexy is what smart guys do.

What good would that guy's ivy-covered education do him if the answer were as simple as the one I gave him?

Erle would know exactly what I was saying.

Those 1,000 evangelists out there going door-to-door, across the continent, calling on the customers – who are, after all, real people, real human beings and not a consumer, not a market, not a demographic, not a research statistic, but a really, really real person – well, that would fit Erle Dardick to a T.

That's what makes dumb guys so smart.

They see the extraordinary in the ordinary.

They see the power of the simple, unvarnished truth.

They see that you don't have to be smart to make gazillion dollars; you simply have to see the truth. And then do something about it!

And it's looking at you every single day.

It's the dust on your desk, the paper slopping around on top of your filing cabinet.

It's the blown-out light bulb on your old sign, telling your customer, the guy driving by, that you're all but out of business; you simply haven't pulled the plug yet.

It's the cheap blue wrinkled sports jacket, long past its prime, that your sales manager wears, just to parody the dress code you proudly created once upon a time when your business was new, when you were dumb enough to be enthusiastic and to think details mattered. Almost like saying, "Your dress code is dumb." And of course it is. Dumb, dumb, dumb.

But that isn't all.

It's the surly waiter, the dirty floor, the menu that once was new but isn't anymore.

It's the kids you hire, or the really, really smart people you recruit out of business school, none of them having any idea how smart the dumb guys who make so much money really are – dumb enough to be passionate about the simple, small details of ordinary things that make the difference in an ordinary world, in which dumb things done well outdo all the smart things done badly, every single time, and by a mile.

And best of all, it doesn't take a smart guy to do it.

No, dumb works just fine, as far as I'm concerned.

And believe it or not, ladies and gentlemen, Erle is about the dumbest guy I know. Because he's taken a really dumb idea like catering, and demystified it so even a smart guy can understand it and have the cartoon light bulb start to glow over his head, and say, "Hey! I could do that, too!" And if you're reading this (and you are) then you're very possibly dumb enough to be hugely successful and make yourself mountains of money, just by putting Erle's remarkable, dumb catering concepts to work.

I hope you are.

Enjoy!

Tom Feltenstein, Chief Executive Officer for *Tom Feltenstein's Power of Marketing Academy*

Tom is a renowned keynote speaker, motivator, trainer, and strategist. A widely praised author, he has written 13 books, including *Change is Good... You Go First, Uncommon Wisdom, NS The Ten Minute Marketer's Secret Formula* (the definitive textbook on Neighborhood Marketing). Tom's latest book is titled *501 Killer Promotional Tactics to Increase Sales, Maximize Profits and Stomp Your Competition.*

**Catering will provide us
with a new revenue channel.**

FOREWORD

by Paul Barron

When Erle asked me to write this foreword I excitingly agreed. The ideas Erle presents in this book go far beyond catering. Though the core of this book's purpose is to grow catering sales and leverage your operations, there are fundamental principles throughout the book that are applicable to anyone within a restaurant or hospitality business.

I began Fastcasual.com in the 90's because I caught trends in the way consumers were interacting with restaurants. I then narrowed my focus to the fast food and casual dining restaurants. The message consumers were sending was clear to me, but others in our industry at the time were hesitant to accept my findings. It took 13 years to get Fast Casual accepted as a major industry segment. Had I let go of the trends I had forecasted, like others had suggested, someone else would undoubtedly be writing this foreword today.

A leader's responsibility is to identify the trends that can impact their business before they actually happen. Forecasting defines proactive leadership; responding to market pressures does not. As the "Great One" Wayne Gretzky said, "A good hockey player plays where the puck is. A *great* hockey player plays where the puck is going to be." So I ask you a simple question: do you want to be a good leader, or do you want to be a great leader?

Discovering hidden profits and unexplored opportunities can make a business amazingly successful. If we analyze the story of Chipotle Mexican Grill and the reasons why they are dominating the Fast Casual segment it becomes immediately obvious. Remember Baja Fresh? Wendy's acquired Baja Fresh in 2002 and sold it in 2006 under the hope that it would follow the same path of Chipotle and McDonald's. So why did Baja Fresh not end up in the same situation as Chipotle? Per my observations, Chipotle's mission was clear; the brand stood for and uncovered the idea of ingredients that were "better for you." This unique branding opportunity was the trick into consumer's hearts and minds. Baja Fresh could have easily been the wonder-boy of the Fast Casual segment, but they missed the mark at a very critical time for the American consumer.

Timing Is Crucial–But Velocity Rules

Timing is what makes us soar or makes us crash. Sometimes we are put in precarious situations with our operations; we are advised to maintain the status quo, keep it comfortable or to just stay the course. In some cases keeping it safe works pretty well. Over the past three decades however, something has changed in our community. Something has caused us to re-assess how we build our brands, our teams and our relationships. This something is called *velocity*! This is simply how fast you bring your ideas into action. It is velocity that has helped the small-fries of technology become the major global powers of today's business world. How did Facebook position itself as the social media power faster than Google? How did Google fail to emerge in the area of social media? I think the answer is simple – speed to market. Facebook had velocity.

The restaurant business and social media are floating in similar waters. Why are countless other brands within Fast Casual winning in a marketplace dominated by much more powerful restaurant brands? I always revert back to what a college coach told me – "Speed is the great equalizer." Knowing when to apply speed will make any brand a force in the industry.

As I previously mentioned, a leader must see where the puck is heading and understand how to leverage their team and assets with a little velocity; this will get a business in a position to win big. *Winning big* is where this book comes in. Erle guides his readers through improving operations in their businesses via the use of catering systems and by developing a more complex program. As Erle suggests in the pages ahead, catering is an area the restaurant industry should be taking advantage of.

Consumer Options

Business leaders today are faced with so many challenges in dealing with the competition. The pure power of choice that consumers have today is immense and the playing field is leveled with tools like social media. Consumers today are savvy and can be utilized as a business' most important tool. Today's consumer is not your average Joe. In fact, the Internet has played a big role in how a consumer gets their information; access to information is faster and variety is everywhere.

With lifestyles being more fragmented and various markets offering consumers immediate options, we have a generation of consumers that is always on – and always seeking a choice.

This is where catering comes in!

Catering can provide relief from the intensity of an office's daily grind. Catering can work for a house party or small get together. Catering changes things up and offers spontaneity. Spontaneity can play a big role in how we connect with consumers. There is a whole, untouched market of consumers who crave this spontaneity and are waiting for our industry to address their needs; we just have to seize the opportunity and take advantage of it.

Consumers are more social now than ever before thanks to Twitter, Facebook, Foursquare and the like. They have many more options readily available to them. As our community faces these new trends, we must see them as opportunities to forge invaluable connections with consumers who are seeking options that we have not been focusing on. This amazing opportunity to cater, to transplant a brand into a home or office, is right within our grasp. Catering is the one solution that can physically bring the brand right to a conference room table or to our backyard get-togethers. It amazes me how few operators do catering well. Yet when we do decide to do something really well, the opportunity to advance is pretty clear.

That is what *Get Catering and Grow Sales!* is all about. Enjoy the pages ahead; I promise that it will be time well invested.

Enjoy the book!

Paul Barron

Webpreneur & Producer - Founder of Fast Casual.com - QSRweb.com, Fast Casual Magazine, The Fast Casual Executive Summit and The Fast Casual Alliance (now known as the Fast Casual Council).

Some things we believe in at MonkeyMedia Software

B e c a u s e
taking the order is the easy
part. We believe in keeping it simple.   We Work Hard.
We Play Hard. We Believe in Giving. We Love to Share Ideas. We Like
Bananas. We like to collaborate. We don't always say yes. We don't always
say no. We're not shy! We believe in ourselves. We go the extra mile. We
believe in service. We train hard. We believe in good health. We believe in kindness. We want
to succeed. We see our clients' success as ours. We believe in having fun. We got here through
hard work and perseverance. We are passionate about our brand. We are passionate about our
clients' brands. We believe that we are the best at what we do. We're honest. We believe in working
effectively. We are good at time management. We are highly organized. We have great controls.
We are responsible. We believe in our people. We believe in love. We believe in peace. We
believe in happiness. We believe in work/life balance. We like to eat well. We believe
in making it right for our clients. We believe that transferring knowledge is
the key to getting it right. We believe the food industry is amazing. We are
entrepreneurial. We believe in making it happen. We believe in fitness. We
believe in working at our relationships. We are accountable to
our stakeholders, and that includes our clients. We do not take
our jobs for granted. We do not take our clients for granted.
We believe in providing opportunity. We believe in creating
opportunity. We believe in sustainability. We believe in
giving back to our community. We have a long
term outlook. We like to have fun. We are
nice people. We're Serious!

PREFACE

By Erle Dardick, MBA, CEO MonkeyMedia Software

The ideas presented in *Get Catering and Grow Sales!* are not mine alone. I am fortunate to have been given the opportunity in my career to spend time thinking about these ideas and concepts. They've been developed during the last 15 years through discussion with other multi-unit restaurant industry professionals and through the ongoing efforts of creating my own vision for the multi-unit restaurant community.

This vision developed out of a deli that I owned and operated. But that story will be told in the pages ahead. Truth is, it's been a long road to get here, and my software story is very grassroots; it is only now that I feel I am able to communicate this vision clearly to you, because of the work we continue to do at MonkeyMedia Software.

At MonkeyMedia Software, our team of industry experts in the multi-unit restaurant catering space, with our fantastic team of implementation and technical specialists, succeed in helping our clients grow their catering businesses through the adoption and investment in our high-level business strategy, our catering education services, and our software as a service (SaaS) model. The software is the last step in our community's catering rollout process, and is used as a tool to help organizations to execute different variations of the strategies that I will put forward in *Get Catering and Grow Sales!*

I wish to make it clear that this is a book about driving new and incremental sales for our community's brands. It's about setting out a roadmap for the future of how our industry can come together as a group and use *Get Catering and Grow Sales!* as a compass for innovating as a community. It's about leveraging our assets to maximize catering as a substantial revenue channel in the multi-unit restaurant environment.

I feel so fortunate to be in this industry and to have been given the trust of many of our colleagues already, to work on their businesses alongside their teams, using our skills, knowledge, passion and technology. Because of this good fortune, I do feel that I have a personal obligation to share my thoughts on how I see the future of this segment of our industry.

From my perspective, all of these ideas belong to our community of multi-unit restaurant operators, and each of you are entitled to receive the benefits of what we have discovered at MonkeyMedia Software. I invite you to integrate the concepts presented here into your daily practices as multi-unit restaurant operators. I sincerely hope that as a group, we will work on making ourselves better and reach our potential in the catering service channel.

I dedicate this book to all our shareholders, executives, managers and frontline employees; people who spend their energy making our multi-unit restaurant community thrive.

Your commitment to our industry is second to none and you all deserve success in your careers and ventures. I hope you find these ideas and perspectives helpful in your daily battles as our industry continues to grow and adapt in the years to come.

Get Catering and Grow Sales! is intended to provide a venue for stimulating more conversation and to create more innovative ideas and direction in our joint task of continuing to both please our guests and adapt to their ever-changing needs.

The multi-unit restaurant community will move into the catering business in a big way because of the shift in consumer culture, as well as the shift in dynamics we have faced as operators over the last 30 years.

Many parts of the North American markets are saturated – and the big brands are going overseas to grow their sales. But as they're doing this, and incurring the accompanying explicit and implicit costs, they are not making the most of the opportunities that are still at home, in catering. The multi-unit restaurant community needs to define additional services at home for their already existing clientele in order to maximize the use of the mature assets and goodwill that we have already established as a community over many decades. And if these practices are established well, then this new service model can be scaled overseas as those markets also begin to mature over the next four or five decades.

Although this discussion can go into many aspects of how to leverage our brands across new sales channels, I have chosen to focus on defining the channel of catering sales for reasons that will become clear. These potential catering sales are low-hanging fruit. I am certain that if we group together, and invest together, we will all benefit. But we will have to stop and take the time to really make sure we understand it, so that we mitigate our risk as we venture into this unknown territory.

As you read on, consider the evolution of our industry over the last century. In the beginning, there were independent operators. This was followed by expansion of some independents into multi-unit operators. Then came the expansion of the corporate build-out model. Once the business logic proved out and systems and technology caught up, our industry moved on to expansion through franchising. As this model gained traction, the technology improved and operators became more sophisticated.

Consider the revenue channel of drive-thru for the QSR segment over the last several decades. In order to shift that consumer behavior, it required innovation and awareness, retooling as operators for guaranteed service execution, and new innovation and investment in technology. Just ask guys like Tom Feltenstein and Ed Rensi. They were there. They invented it. There was no drive-thru channel before that. All these years later, drive-thru revenue represents a lion's share of our community's revenues. Nobody could have predicted that. The same thing happened with breakfast under their management. Through their great leadership it became a standard for many brands, and our industry grew.

I want to bring to your attention that in *Get Catering and Grow Sales!* I propose that catering is the next natural top-line growth channel for our multi-unit restaurant industry.

Consider this our beginning together as we grow the concept of business-to-business catering into an exciting revenue channel opportunity for our entire community. I hope this book will help to frame this conversation for our sector in the years to come.

Once the ideas and concepts in this book become part of the public domain, if I am fortunate, we will see our competitors at MonkeyMedia Software continue to grow and develop these ideas. I consider all our technology providers to be part of our community as well and I expect them to push the technology for our industry to the limits. I am certain that when this happens, it will be good for everyone who holds a stake in our industry, including my own software company.

And so, I am putting this out there in the hopes that we will all take the time to share and discuss *Get Catering and Grow Sales!* in our boardrooms and at industry conferences.

I recognize the potential conflicts of interest between brands that could arise in this market, as there are some brands that are already having success in this segment. I urge those operators that feel this potential conflict of interest, to open their hearts and use their intellectual capacity for the greater good of our community. If they do so, they will help to keep us unified and moving forward towards a shared goal of growing top-line sales for our entire industry. In the end, that will prove to be beneficial for everyone.

Please join me in this conversation and send me your thoughts as you read through the pages ahead. The ideas in this manuscript originate from my passion and experience in this field. I hope we get an opportunity to work hard on these concepts together for many years to come.

Sincerely,

Erle

Sitting in a quiet catering space

I invite you to sit with me quietly in your brand's "catering space." It begins in our imagination. No office noise, no interruptions.

Imagine what the catering channel can do for your business, both in the immediate sense and in the long term. Focus on how we get your brand to achieve up to $1,000 per day, Monday - Friday in incremental catering sales, for each one of your stores that does catering, in locations where catering makes sense.

Don't get stuck on the "why nots" at this point and time. There is time later to address that.

In this quiet space, I want to explore the subtleties and potential pitfalls of what you might expect to come across as you scale these ideas throughout your existing infrastructure.

Once you feel that you can imagine the big-picture opportunity for your brand, ignoring the details of "how" for the moment, we can discuss the subtleties and considerations, and make the strategic decision of whether or not your brand should service the catering revenue channel.

Once you begin to get comfortable with the potential of the concepts, you will be in a position to make the right decision for your brand as well as understand the commitment required for you to succeed in this market.

Ok... back to all the noise now... phones ringing, problems with orders, customers complaining, marketing campaigns.

I just couldn't sit here and watch anymore! So, I wrote instead!

As we know, in business, we live or die by our professional commitment. That is it. If we take on a catering strategy for our brands, we have a duty to protect the goodwill that we have worked so hard to earn from our customers over the years. Brand goodwill is lost very quickly in the catering channel if this professional commitment is not respected.

There is an implicit challenge, from a brand goodwill perspective, in catering: we execute the order internally but our guest experience for catering is outside our four walls.

Too many of us are meeting this expectation half-way. I see many of us going forward blindly with catering with no plan and no assessment as to the impact that the growth of this channel will have on our existing operations.

I want to help prevent this from continuing. There are billions of dollars on the table in getting our catered meals onto the tables of our customers in a predictable and scalable way. There are billions of dollars to be lost if we continue to do it with the wrong business logic and the lack of understanding of how to service this market properly.

One of my key objectives for writing *Get Catering and Grow Sales!* is to slow us down as a community when it comes to thinking about what catering means for our brands and have us thinking instead about what it *could* mean.

I want to provide a valuable and alternative perspective on a real-world business challenge, plus a look at the long-term challenge facing multi-unit restaurant operators. This is part of the larger debate as to why the catering revenue channel will be required for the survival of all brands in the years ahead.

I do not plan to name any industry brands because my concepts for catering are "brand agnostic." It's the business logic and organizational business structure that I propose is critically important for our community at large.

Another aim of this book is to provide the language and concepts needed in order to move forward as internal champions as it relates to catering for our brands. We must really understand how this channel can positively impact the sales of our industry to the tune of many billions of dollars. These dollars will be critical to the long-term survival of all of our brands.

I chuckle to myself as I write this because here I am trying to convince the smartest people in our multi-unit restaurant community that they have been missing this and that somehow I figured it out.

I want to go on record here, that I'm not that smart! I simply got lucky at getting the opportunity to apply these ideas at Tony's Deli, and the results were positive all the way around. Please don't misunderstand. It took an incredible amount of work and commitment to get Tony's Deli to where it is today.

If you had spent a day at the deli with me in the old days, you'd be chuckling, too!

As the CEO of MonkeyMedia Software, while writing *Get Catering and Grow Sales!* I struggled with the idea of being perceived as trying to push our community towards using our software to help service this catering revenue channel.

This book is simply meant to serve our entire community and _not sell software_. The challenge I have here is that because our software is built around the perspective that I am going to share with you as we continue, the intellectual property captured in our technology is the same as that captured in this book. I decided to proceed anyway, because I am genuinely excited by these concepts, and I hope that as a community, we will take these ideas and make them ours. There is a lot of work to do for all of us moving forward if these revenues are to be realized.

Catering just happens to be a channel that I really enjoy thinking and talking about, because I have experienced the results personally and continue to see others take advantage of the hidden opportunity. They, too, are getting fantastic results.

Our community needs to proceed thoughtfully and responsibly as we consider the growth of North America's most successful food service and restaurant brands and how to leverage them across more revenue channels.

I needed to write _Get Catering and Grow Sales!_ to keep the discussion flowing, because each of us, as a multi-unit restaurant executive, is faced with the same challenges. The challenge we especially share is that we _all need to drive more sales._

There are three parts to the book and each can be read separately; Part One is the Story, Part Two is the Theory and Part Three contains the details of what needs to happen in our operations to execute the strategy with precision and confidence. It focuses on business structure for catering and the roles and responsibilities that have to get filled. Part Three is targeted towards our multi-unit restaurant managers, who need to execute against the strategy that is decided upon by our executive teams.

It is very important to discuss and challenge the perspectives being put forward here. By doing so, as a group, we will be able to grow this perspective for the entire community, arriving at a better place together.

Credit where credit is due

I have shared the ideas in this book with so many great operators, and the culmination of these discussions are all in _Get Catering and Grow Sales!_ I am grateful to have been given this gift in my career, to be able to focus in on a single transformative idea for our industry, along with the support of so many believers.

Because I have been a personal benefactor of these ideas, I feel I owe this work to our community so that you too may use these ideas to make your businesses better.

I have thought long and hard as to why, in the entire U.S., there are only a handful of national multi-unit brands that are doing catering well. In every case, these companies are generating anywhere from a low of $30 million to a high of $150 million in incremental catering revenue sales per year.

Why is this the case? Why only a handful of national brands?

These brands have made a deep commitment to the business of catering, and they have a clear vision of what the catering revenue channel looks like for their own brand. In addition, each of them is making investments into their own catering experience and putting in the effort required to make it happen. It touches deep within the core values of the company, and is a major part of their company culture.

Of course, many of them have room for operational and systems improvement, but they have managed to grow a substantial revenue channel across existing assets where others have not.

I would like to pause here for a moment to congratulate them for their vision, commitment and success. I am aware that given they are such an important part of our growth as a community, they too will benefit from the concepts in *Get Catering and Grow Sales!*

I want to clarify for these operators, that if they too share their knowledge and agree to be part of ongoing conversations within our community, then they will also see their sales grow in this segment. To that end, I would like to invite these operators to join this conversation. They will gain great strength as organizations and help pave the way for our future together.

Each of these operators should be on our community's "Catering Council for Multi-Unit Food Service Operators" (CCMUFSO) to help guide legislation and new innovation.

Catering in the years ahead

I am certain that in the years ahead, the impact of the catering revenue channel will be felt deeply in our industry boardrooms. I see it happening every day, more and more. As the numbers from this growing sector begin to present themselves, we will all work hard to discover new and creative ways to drive more sales and we will create more discussion inside our organizations as we continue to learn how the catering revenue channel will impact our brands.

We will engage suppliers, including our technology partners, in this discussion as well, because more top-line sales for us results in more top-line sales for them. They need to understand and get invested in these concepts in the early stages.

Executing catering profitably will continue to be a good use of idle capacity and will help to maximize the return on the assets which we have already deployed and paid for in our existing infrastructure over the last four or five decades.

I believe that catering strategies should be looked at for our brands that are suffering financially because catering sales can be the difference between losing and making money at the unit level. This is specifically true for marginal units, where sales are declining and costs are rising.

Catering will play into the ability of all brands to provide corporate services and continue to build loyalty within the corporate community. This, in turn, will present an opportunity where multi-unit restaurant operators can really penetrate the buying influence of our

Imagine if we take the professional step of establishing an industry authority, such as the 'Catering Council for Multi-Unit Restaurant Operators' (CCMURO), and put a stamp of approval on our community's catering operations.

Imagine the CCMURO, conceived in the process of writing Get Catering and Grow Sales!, how fun would that be?

The CCMURO best-practices board would provide brands with a "stamp of approval" for providing a safe and thoughtfully-executed guest experience. We would need to find ways to measure ourselves against the standards and expectations agreed upon as a group.

consumers. With our great messaging and our customers' brand loyalty it only makes sense that we should sell to them at their place of business.

If we can reach our customers at their places of work, as well as offer them additional services, we have just extended our customer reach and increased the probability for repeat business – not to mention the increase in brand awareness. Of course, the major assumption I am making here is that we actually take ourselves seriously in this channel.

There is a lot to consider here prior to popping up those catering marketing posters in the windows of our stores. There are hundreds of decisions that need to be made first in order to align us internally to guarantee a successful outcome.

Once these ideas are fully integrated into our company cultures and our people's knowledge, we will come to understand why this channel is so exciting! I hope we will develop a deep appreciation and respect for the organizational commitment required to guarantee success. We need to understand the consequences and long-term risks our industry faces if we decide to continue to treat catering as an "add-on business".

In order to support the growth in these catering sales, each of us will need to make room organizationally, but we will be happy to do so when those catering sales are coming in the door.

At MonkeyMedia Software, the operators that we see having any degree of success in growing their catering sales channel are the ones that are investing resources into growing it. They spend a lot of time, money and energy on trying to figure out how to do it. Then, once they do, they scale it rapidly across their existing infrastructure.

They are committed from the top down. Period. This is probably the single most important idea you can take away from *Get Catering and Grow Sales! Strategy, strategy, strategy!*

The organizations that we work with that have this commitment, and are following their strategies, are experiencing top-line catering sales growth, rapidly. Through our strategy services, education work and our software, their order execution is flawless and their catering customer satisfaction is high. This is yielding repeat catering transactions. The customers' relationship with the brand is growing and their trust in the brand is even higher. These organizations are making their customers look good and those customers are coming back for more of everything. I will discuss the reasons why this is the case in-depth, later on in Parts Two and Three of *Get Catering and Grow Sales!*

As we continue together, feel free to skip around to the topics that are of particular interest. I begin with my personal story to provide some background.

PART I – The Story

Need a turn-around strategy?

Try catering.

Tony's Deli and Catering Company
1046 Commercial Drive,
Vancouver, BC, Canada

Tony's Deli (1996), where my foodservice venture began

My first interaction with Tony's Deli was as a customer. This delicatessen is famous in Vancouver for its Panini (Italian pressed and fresh sandwiches), baked goods, coffee, and fantastic-tasting foods. It is a popular, long-established institution in East Vancouver's Italian district on Commercial Drive. It was already 25 years old when I got involved, and had changed owners six or seven times in two-and-a-half decades, but each owner had kept the name. It had the feel and reputation of a well-loved family business. Tony Barrucci is the original owner from 1972. He and I met on several occasions over the years and he was always proud that his name was still on the awning. Tony retired from the food business and now teaches ballroom dancing. You can still feel his passion and energy inside the four walls of the Deli on Commercial drive.

I was already a successful entrepreneur with seven businesses behind me by the time I was 30. While working outside the food industry, I had decided to go back to school to get an MBA for my own personal development. The campus for Simon Fraser University's business school was located in downtown Vancouver. Tony's Deli was located midway between my office and the campus. On Tuesdays and Thursdays I would arrive at the deli around 5 p.m., work on my assignments, and enjoy the food and coffee until classes started at 7:30 p.m.

At the time that I became involved with the deli, Tony's was owned and operated by another entrepreneur who was an exceptional food retailer. In addition, he had previous food business experience in the kitchen and a wonderful palate, which he used for his Panini creations. He was a strong customer service guy, always pleasant to be around, and he had this knack for getting people in the door.

At the time, Tony's Deli was thriving, with good volume in its retail channel. The one weak link was operations and the all-around business strategy. The systems and controls in place at the time needed strengthening and it was clear that my skill set could add value to the equation as David (the owner of Tony's) and I got to know each other over time.

David was always interested in my MBA studies and he had really big ideas for Tony's Deli. His passion was fierce, and we shared numerous interesting chats about his plans. As I was transitioning between businesses and looking for an interesting project to work on, he hired me as a consultant to work four days per week, and this became my entry (15 years ago) into this fascinating food industry.

In 1997, after six months of consulting and uncovering many skeletons in the closet, I decided to take an ownership position and restructured the company by rolling the assets into a new company. From there, we went back to the beginning and the basics of what had made Tony's Deli so special.

I'll save the war stories, but my life became pretty much dedicated to that deli and each morning I arrived with the attitude to improve it, to service our customers and to continue to find new ways to drive sales.

As the days passed, many customers would ask us if we could bring the "Tony's Experience" to their offices. "Of course!" we would tell them. After all, we were entrepreneurs! We never turned down business as long as we believed

A Budding Entrepreneur

The Early Entrepreneurial Years

As an entrepreneur, I like to start new things, find a good idea and go with it. This started early for me.

When it snowed in the winter when I was a kid in Montreal, I would grab my shovel, knock on doors and shovel walks. Sometimes I would even shovel first and then knock. But one morning my neighbor, Mrs. Garland, scolded me for not asking for her permission first… She kindly gave me a quarter anyway because she was happy with my work.

Later, when I was 18, I bought leather goods from bankrupt manufacturers with a friend, and sold them on to a local chain of leather goods stores. I asked the buyer how many he wanted as we had hundreds of pieces. He took them all and my first real business transaction was complete. I had caught the entrepreneurial bug.

we could execute on our commitment to our customers. It was with this beginning that we offered our products and services to our local corporate market.

This was the start of the business-to-business catering service at Tony's Deli. Of course, there was always the demand for personal catering services as well, however, I decided strategically that I wanted Tony's Deli to be a category killer for both the corporate breakfast and lunch market because I believed at the time that it was the simplest to scale.

When we started, it became quickly apparent that our systems needed refining. At first, we took orders on a napkin. The wind would blow and we'd lose an order! Shortly after, we created a standard manual form. This at least put some structure into the questions we were asking our customers during the order entry process so that we could use the data to execute. Of course, in those days we would key the order into the register system and then we'd execute the orders manually.

As we got better at our catering service, sales grew quickly. We became very good at the enterprise; our products were fresh, we were known for a strong customer service experience, and we were hands-on and consistent with our catering each and every day.

Looking back now, the most important learning for me was how we managed to leverage our retail location and brand, and to grow these sales out the back door of the deli. We refined our services and focused our attention on creating a customer experience for the boardroom table. We looked at every aspect of our operations, including our commitment to sticking to our flavor profile at the same time adjusting portion sizes and innovating our packaging.

Catering sales were growing so quickly, we eventually changed the company's name to "Tony's Deli and **Catering Company**". By then, we had nailed down our menus. We had this fantastic, personalized corrugated cardboard tray package made with our logos on it. We offered two sizes of platter products into the trays. We used these trays for our Paninis (non-grilled), desserts, fruit platters, antipasto platters, cheese platters and so on. If you wanted our grilled Panini program, we defined that as a catering event at Tony's. We'd certainly provide our customers with the experience however, we charged appropriately and executed it differently than our corporate catering drop-off delivery business. It was a different business, from our perspective.

Then it happened. Catering took off like a rocket, and all our systems started to break down. We were caught off guard with the volume of business, and experienced a lot of growing pains.

We had worked so hard to build the Tony's brand in our community, establish relationships, and now, because we were experiencing a sudden and sharp increase in sales volume, the cracks in our system were showing. Mistakes, late orders, missed orders. We were losing the small but important details on some orders, like "No mayo for Frank". As the days passed, the stress at the deli intensified. For personal reasons, my partner sold his interest to me at the deli, and I continued on alone.

Much of my life was wrapped up in Tony's Deli and it was not uncommon for me to work 15- to 17-hour days. Life at the deli was busy; making money took a lot of focus.

We went from strength to strength, developed our operating system through our experience, and between 1998 and 2001 we ramped up our overall annual sales to $2 million. It was only a single store (1,700 sq. feet), and, of course, I was a hands-on operator day in and day out, but these were strong results.

By that time, catering represented 50 percent of Tony's revenue. Another interesting result was that our retail sales were also growing. I began to understand that the cross-pollination of our retail marketing while delivering our catering experience, resulted in building even more brand awareness to consumers that had never heard of Tony's before. Because of the positive catering experience, we were acquiring new fans for the brand!

In order for me to shift our business where we could execute half our sales through catering at that time, we had to buy the business next door (a small sub shop) and convert it into a production kitchen. We also bought a few more trucks and had adjusted and trained our people in how we wanted our service executed. We then had people who were dedicated only to the catering side of our business.

Observing it all, we realized that the "cross-pollination" of customers was a critical factor to driving sales, in all segments. The same customers used our different services, depending on their needs. We became very good at training our front counter staff in the language of catering, and we improved our signage and catering visibility in the store to help drive more catering sales.

We invested in a small sales team as well as in our packaging and marketing. The press noticed us in a positive way, which built up our profile further.

Again, as the days passed, and we continued to look for ways to improve our business, we met another local entrepreneur who had a very tiny business that was focused on web-based animation. His business was named MonkeyMedia. NET.

MonkeyMedia.NET's business had stalled because the owner was an artistic guy and not a great businessman; he had clients, but many were frustrated with him. We decided to combine forces, with myself again in the role of fixing the business side, and MonkeyMedia became part of my business portfolio.

How we put the "software" in MonkeyMedia

While Tony's Deli's successes were increasing, we decided that we would use MonkeyMedia as a vehicle to add technology to our ideas of how to execute our catering. We began to work on a web-based back-end system to manage the burgeoning catering business. We took our time, worked on it very carefully every day, in between other MonkeyMedia customers.

As we developed the tool over the web, we would use it at Tony's when the phones would ring for a catering order. We'd key orders in, generate invoices, process credit cards and also provide for online ordering. The system developed by MonkeyMedia continued to evolve around the needs of Tony's Deli for almost five years. We had worked our recipes in, our vendors, costs, and, of course, all of our catering production and delivery data. It was the byword in efficiency.

By the time we hit 2001, Tony's Deli was squeezing 51 percent gross margins after raw materials, paper and labor. With $2 million in sales, we had a very strong business and I attribute a lot of that growth to the technology we were developing for servicing our catering customers.

My knack for fixing businesses came in handy now. MonkeyMedia had no real focus back then, but one was becoming apparent. We had developed a great SaaS-based software tool for Tony's Deli and so the owner of MonkeyMedia and I became partners in a venture where we added the word "Software" to the name, with the idea that we would focus our software products on the food business.

The food business became my area of expertise and the technology, though clunky at that time, worked well for my deli. In retrospect, I can see how MonkeyMedia Software developed as we took on a client here and a client there. We continued to apply our skills to other food businesses, and although we didn't know exactly what the outcome would be, we were a few guys who loved the food business and were having fun trying to figure it out. Certainly, we understood business well and we had some coding skills, but we never considered the software's scalability in those days; the ability to cope with and accommodate growth.

At the time, MonkeyMedia Software was a side project for both my partner and myself. It was mostly a "fun" venture that we were playing with. The software was accidentally developed to solve the real-life challenges of catering out of a deli. Because of this, the intellectual property and ideas that were documented into the software were unique to our situation and our perspective.

We were processing and executing all our orders, invoicing, payments, production and distribution with this web-based tool we had created for Tony's Deli. Business was humming at the deli, and I decided on a personal level that I had so much more passion for the food industry as a whole. I was hungry for more learning and, as such, made the decision to sell Tony's while it was on top, so that I could venture down the path of MonkeyMedia Software full-time.

Since the sale of Tony's Deli in 2006, MonkeyMedia Software has successfully shaped and deployed the same strategy with other operators. It continues to work, especially as we scale it in larger multi-unit operators. Our clients are all streamlining and growing their catering businesses successfully.

How MonkeyMedia Software became an industry leader

I have to roll back to 1999 to describe how others began to appreciate our work. Tony's was doing great. Then, in 2001, amid the turmoil after 9/11 and local political developments that impacted the general business climate, the markets fell drastically and business at Tony's Deli took a sharp decline over previous years.

By March 2002, business was down 20 percent over the previous year. While there was some relief that it wasn't just my company in this position, I watched with huge concern as some of my neighbors went out of business. Even though business was slow, I considered myself lucky to still be going.

Looking for a creative solution to the challenge, I picked up the phone and called The Spectra Group of Great Restaurants, owners of a Vancouver restaurant chain called the Bread Garden Bakery and Cafe. I knew little about them and had never met their executives, but I figured they might be interested in our now-refined software for their business.

After leaving many messages for Peter Bonner, their CEO, I finally received a call back from their VP of operations, Mark Roberts. I invited Mark to Tony's Deli and showed him what we were doing at Tony's Deli as well as the back-end of the software that had been created by MonkeyMedia Software.

This meeting ultimately landed us the opportunity to work closely with Peter, Mark and Dick Benmore, Spectra's CFO, to help them transition a commissary they owned onto our platform; it was more for manufacturing than catering but, being entrepreneurs, we gave it a go.

We proceeded to work on their commissary for the following four months and successfully deployed our software into their operations. In practical terms, this resulted in moving a $12 million per year factory into a web-based manufacturing environment.

Now we, as owners of MonkeyMedia Software, were in the software business for the food industry, and we proceeded to pursue this idea of getting more clients in Vancouver and Seattle. We continued to have success in this trial-and-error phase for the company. We were learning a great deal.

As MonkeyMedia Software went to market with two software solutions—multi-unit restaurant catering and food manufacturing—we continued to acquire customers for our Software as a Service (Saas) model.

As the success of MonkeyMedia Software intensified, I decided to divest myself of Tony's Deli in 2006 to concentrate full time to what was becoming the vision for my personal work in the food industry. We were having a major impact on our customers' businesses at a strategic level, and bringing sophisticated technology to a technologically unsophisticated industry. In 2007, my MonkeyMedia Software partner left the company to pursue other interests.

It was another transitional time that brought with it an opportunity to take MonkeyMedia Software to the next level. In 2007, MonkeyMedia Software brought in a professional management team to help provide software and strategies for catering in the multi-unit restaurant environment.

If you are not catering, you're leaving a lot of money on the table.

We will lead the way for the world's multi-unit restaurant brands – big and small

With strategy, education, and technology, we are in a unique position to provide this knowledge and leadership to the world's biggest brands in the food service industry. Of course, these concepts can also be adopted by our smaller brands in the multi-unit restaurant community; however, we will know that when our big brands are executing catering well, our industry will have grown. As such, we will all grow with them.

At MonkeyMedia Software, we intend to be specifically and thoughtfully influential in the community of multi-unit restaurant operators, as it relates to helping them drive their own catering revenue. Each of us is in a position to grow our North American sales in this segment.

We believe that through our work at MonkeyMedia Software we are helping to set the standards for catering in our industry. The adoption of these practices through awareness, education and technology will change our industry forever.

Everything I write in *Get Catering and Grow Sales!* comes from the perspective of the guy who owned and operated Tony's Deli. All these ideas, the vision for business-to-business catering on a massive and organized scale, and the software came out of my experiences and my perspectives as an operator.

During the last 15 years, I bought and turned around a deli, revived a multi-unit restaurant and commissary operation as a hired consultant, and grew MonkeyMedia Software to make the food business better.

In each of these turnaround cases, my task was to roll the assets out to a new company structure, pay back the secured creditors, and generally fix the businesses. As a small business guy, I am accustomed to hands-on situations, and I enjoy the challenge of fixing companies that are in distress.

As a serial entrepreneur – MonkeyMedia Software is my 9th business – I became very good at finding the fastest way to profits, assuming there was already a decent sales volume running through the till. It did not matter what the business was; I had an ability to get a quick hold of the costs and figure out how to increase margins and sales. (This is no easy task for those of you who also know how to do this!) Fixing a business with urgency to save it takes a special kind of skill.

As we began to 'fix' Tony's Deli, we developed a strategy that worked very well that contributed a huge impact to the bottom-line of the business. We increased sales-per-square-foot using our existing assets and, at the same time, maintained and even grew our core retail business, which was crucial in maintaining brand equity.

I have spent countless hours doing it, thinking about it, talking about it and making the strategy work for others over the last 15 years, and it continues to be fundamentally sound. And while I no longer own it, Tony's Deli and Catering Company is still succeeding with this strategy in the Vancouver market under new management.

I have learned that it's all about the strategy first – passion and energy second. For each client we take on and work with the situation is different and specific. But we have become specialists at shaping our clients' strategies, with their invitation to do so.

In the long run, this strategy is helping to shape the future of our multi-unit restaurant industry. In many ways, it's not about the software at all. It's more about the strategy, and the successful implementation of that strategy using as much of the current infrastructure as possible. Of course, technology plays a big role in creating a scalable and predictable service experience, but cannot be used until the strategy is well understood and the investment into education and technology is agreed upon. Each of us has to work on our business to experience success. Getting into the catering revenue channel is a serious decision.

Our software was developed as a by-product of a small deli in Vancouver. What drove the development was the strategy of the deli and the need to provide our people with a tool that they could use to execute high customer satisfaction. That was simply by happenstance because, truth be told, I was just trying to run my deli efficiently.

What I know now is that it's the perspective of the business logic and ideas towards that perspective that became so interesting. It just so happens that we captured this perspective and these ideas in web-based software.

All brands, big and small, operate in challenging times

As a group, we are failing to maximize the use of existing assets and the goodwill we have built in our brands over the last several decades, simply because we have not gone through the proper analysis as a community.

We need a shift in culture and perspective.

As brand operators, we have so many burning issues to manage, such as declining same-store sales, human resource issues, landlords to manage, and suppliers to negotiate with, not to mention franchise communities that need more support and services.

Operations are already having all kinds of quality and service issues. Every day is "show business" in our retail environments.

A conversation should be taking place in every one of North America's food service boardrooms, including the entire supply chain for the multi-unit restaurant community. We need to include our distribution channels and our manufacturers so that they too can continue to innovate and make it easier to grow this catering revenue channel. Everyone with a vested interest in this niche community should be discussing the business-to-business catering revenue channel as a revenue growth opportunity in their boardrooms and among their management teams.

There is a market opportunity here that is worth many billions of dollars in incremental revenue for our industry – and we should capitalize on it. We can build additional brand equity for multi-unit restaurant operators while growing sales in this significant way. I am proposing here, that our catering services are not defined well and our execution is poor. A lot of this business is already going to independent operators and grocery delis that know how to do it, and because of the power of our brands, we have a real opportunity to bring many of those dollars in our direction.

When it comes to business-to-business catering, our potential customers are confused by what is currently on offer from multi-unit restaurant operators. We are performing poorly in filling the demand for these services as an industry. If we can mobilize ourselves to service these markets properly we will learn that the opportunity for sales growth and improvement is substantial for the whole industry.

The business model the industry has held on to over the last five decades, of building out more and more brick-and-mortar locations in developed markets, is becoming increasingly difficult, certainly in the North American markets. The reasons are varied: Good locations are hard to find; restrictive legislation, such as that enacted in South Los Angeles to prevent QSR saturation; landlords are more sophisticated and the costs of building out are substantial and rising.

As we are all aware, financial capital continues to be difficult to access, and almost every community that our brands service is saturated with competition. This "perfect storm" makes it difficult to attract new retail customers for established brands in the North American marketplace. Essentially, to stay alive, brands make constant "deal" offers.

Attracting consumers to "our brand" over "other brands" is not generating industry sales growth at any stellar rate. Consumers are not spending more money in total, they are just choosing another brand on a given day, depending on what they are in the mood for. Current consumers are not going to eat more than one lunch today. There is only so much lunch money to go around, at the consumer retail level. The same argument holds true for our other dayparts as well.

Another issue facing our multi-unit restaurant operators, which creates even more of an uphill battle, is that retail price points are very sensitive, and there is constant upward pressure on all raw material and operating costs. The only path to survival for our community is to drive more store traffic and sales. This is not going to be an easy task in the long run, unless we find new sales channels, and work in a unified way to help our whole industry.

Many brands look to expanding in emerging markets such as Asia and India. That is fine, but this international expansion does not solve the dilemma facing so many marginal operators and sluggish sales back at home. Even as we build international markets, eventually they, too, will become saturated and will have to consider catering revenue as a vehicle for top-line sales growth.

Multi-unit restaurant executives have a responsibility to consider all the avenues that can add value to the experience of our brands.

I am proposing here that as a community we can find ways to grow our sales together, in unison. There is a tremendous amount of power in that statement.

Ultimately, additional sales will be driven by consumer demand, but it is the responsibility of our industry to invest in educating customers as to what products and services we have to offer. Should our buyers agree to purchase more services, we then need to ensure that professional standards emerge, to ensure the long-term success of our industry. We need to clearly define our strategy, our policies, our procedures, and we need to make sure we understand the business model when it is scaled across our infrastructure.

Can you imagine? But, who has the time? We're already so busy just trying to get a handle on our current challenges and operations. It will be fascinating to see which brands end up adopting these concepts first and invest in making it work for their own organizations because they believe it's the right strategy.

As an operator, the extension of services to our current customers is often hard to see. Right in front of all of us is a customer who requires more services from our multi-unit restaurant community. We are failing as an industry at explaining and defining the additional services that we can extend to our customers.

This story is familiar and has been told in our nation's restaurant company boardrooms for years. Why does catering continue to stay in the background? Why is catering viewed as an "add-on" business, and not as part of our core business strategy? We are getting closer to answering these questions. I am certain of it!

I want to challenge our community at the executive level: if we have not invested any time into considering business-to-business catering as part of our main brand strategy, then it is wholly possible that we are making a key strategic error in the long run for our brands.

Imagining catering from a brand perspective

In my opinion, "catering" is one of the most loosely defined terms in the hospitality industry, specifically as it relates to defining these services in our multi-unit restaurant community.

As a potential business revenue stream, it continues to be a nagging element, but in many cases it keeps getting pushed to the next quarter due to lack of focus, understanding and resources. It is not well understood. It's just another 'burning issue' as we carry out our daily work.

In the old days, catering was left to the caterers, filling the needs of large-scale private events such as weddings and Bar Mitzvahs – which can take place on or off the restaurant premises. But these days, things are different.

Today, just as all markets in every industry have become more focused on specialty niches, so, too, catering has split into several channels.

The following three types of catering services are what we covered at Tony's Deli and what I would like to focus on as clear definitions in *Get Catering and Grow Sales!* These services can be corporate or private:

- Off-premise drop-off catering with set up service;

- Off-premise drop-off catering without set up service;

- Off-premise catering for pick-up.

As well, we will focus our discussion on the catering revenue channel in the QSR, Fast Casual and Casual-dining segments.

Once we have clarity around our key markets, we can dive into the details of how to create more opportunities for ourselves in these spaces.

I purposely removed custom-event catering from our discussion, such as weddings. Although we can provide a more upscale service level for our brand, and call it the Event Catering Division, it is not a market that is sustainable for the long-term strategy of leveraging current assets to drive incremental sales revenue.

While I do not view the event catering business as a scalable business across any brand, I am not saying it should be ignored. It is yet another business to consider, but not the focus of this book.

Instead, drop-off and pick-up catering as well as staging catering orders onsite as part of the execution process, are extra services that we can charge for – but they need to be well defined by our industry. We have not defined or standardized the catering business option, and as such the lines and definitions are blurred for our operators, technology vendors and our customers.

In *Get Catering and Grow Sales!* I attempt to define this so that everyone in a multi-unit restaurant operator/franchisee/licensee business setting can understand the opportunity on the table and make the right decision for their brand and organization.

Once our customers begin to understand this new "catering language", they will purchase more of these products and services in addition to the ones they are already buying from us.

This is where the power lies; we already have customers who trust our brands, so if we can just look after their additional needs, they will count on us to help them fill the demand that they have for these services.

A hamburger is a sandwich! Sandwiches are great for catering!

Many brands in the hamburger segment, for example, have told us at MonkeyMedia Software that they like the idea of catering, but they can't figure out how to get hot hamburgers to the boardroom and still guarantee the quality and experience of the burger, never mind the fries and hot apple turnovers.

Here is where the fundamental change needs to begin.

We must "get out of the box" in order to see the catering vision for our brands. Defining a catering strategy for a hamburger brand, for example, is the first step.

It might not be about hamburgers at all, but it might be about leveraging the hamburger brand across other products that are more "catering friendly". Because the catering service is being offered by that hamburger brand, demand will come because of the power of the brand itself, and the trust that it has already earned over the years from its broad customer base. If our operators create the right experience for our brands, our customers will buy these services from us just because they love and trust us already. They will remain loyal.

Catering should be part of the overall strategy initiative for ALL multi-unit restaurant operators. It all begins with the strategic vision at the leadership level.

If, in general, we agree that growing top-line sales for our brands using existing infrastructure will positively impact the cash flow and profitability of our industry, then why aren't more of us doing catering in our food businesses? And why have others tried and failed?

You might think: "Ok Erle, if there is such a big market out there, then why aren't the phones ringing more for these services? For example, why don't the largest hamburger chains in the world get any calls for catering?"

Don't they?

I am certain that if the world's largest hamburger brands made a strategic decision to grow their catering sales in their existing markets it would be very powerful for their top line sales. This statement holds true for any multi-unit restaurant operator, because of the way we are structured. However, I am making a huge assumption here that we understand what has to be done to achieve success in this market.

If, in fact, it is all about using the power of the brand to drive new revenue channels, then imagine what will happen when the biggest brands in the world make a strategic decision to be in the catering business.

The big challenge in terms of making the most of potential catering sales, would be that our industry does not have the expertise or understand the business model well enough to venture outside the box that far. Not yet that is. It's not that we don't see the opportunity it's just that we don't want to work so hard on something that we don't understand very well. But when we do finally get it and decide strategically to invest in it, can you imagine the incremental sales revenue?

The phones are not going to ring for catering today, because many of us have not developed the strategy required to make the phones ring. It's that simple. The strategy is missing.

Here is my big tip for those who are in the burger business and have hit flat sales growth in stores, or at best, are only seeing very small incremental increases; If you are toying with catering in the back of your mind, stop thinking about hot burgers, fries and milkshakes on the boardroom table. It's not about that menu. *It's about creating a new brand experience*, with catering-friendly products, along with following the best practices of growing and executing services in this revenue channel.

To create this brand experience we will need to be very creative. We will need to start at the beginning. *Start with the menu.*

Make catering part of your core business!

Catering is a hidden revenue channel for most of us in the multi-unit restaurant community.

We're not ignoring it, but mostly we are just fighting so many other fires, we just can't seem to get to it. It's not yet part of our core businesses, and it needs to be for the long-run success of our industry.

It is my hope, that as multi-unit restaurant executives, we will be able to discuss and consider these ideas in order to create more dialogue inside our companies, especially in the boardroom, of how to successfully take our brands outside our four walls and into our communities, by providing more excellent services to our customers.

By doing so, we will grow additional value from within that will generate more revenue and more profits for our brands. This allows us to continue to invest in ourselves in the years to come. Through those investments and the work and energy of our people and our community, we will make positive change in our industry by making it grow.

Catering is a serious business!

As I travel around the U.S. and Canada visiting the boardrooms of some of the most successful brands in our industry, I perceive a change slowly taking place.

The idea of taking catering seriously as its own business and rolling it out throughout America's major brands, both in the corporate and franchised systems, is just now gaining understanding. However, these are still early days. I feel very lucky to be part of the discussion and to be initiating and encouraging work on these ideas.

Although catering can represent 20% of overall system sales, it can contribute more than 40% of overall gross margin.

We Do What It Takes

Catering is a very dynamic business: it's changing, it's moving, and details get forgotten. You need to be able to talk about these things, to communicate, to know what to do when these things go wrong; you need to train your people for these times of stress. Once, at Tony's, we were feeding the executives at a large local telecom company in Vancouver called Telus and my driver got there and called me up after he locked his keys in the van.

The food was due upstairs in five minutes and it was the last delivery of the day. I instructed him to smash the window (which would not touch the food as it was a truck divided in the interior) and to deliver the food to our hungry customers. He followed my lead and carried out our duty to the customer without a hitch.

The moral of the story for me is one of professionalism. If we hadn't smashed that window, which maybe cost $200 to repair, I would have ended up with 40 high-powered people in the boardroom feeling very frustrated with my brand. Clearly the dollars lost by losing the customer would have been much greater than the repair of the broken window. Servicing the customer is always the priority!

In the next 10 years, catering will be the fastest sales-growth opportunity for our multi-unit restaurant community, I am certain of this. Catering will grow as did drive-thru and breakfast before it. It's easy to get into it once you know how.

While, our industry needs additional research on how the catering revenue channel can impact our brands, our operations, and the overall financial health of our systems, I am confident that once the successes of these strategies are well documented, catering will be further integrated into brand operations as a standard moving forward in the years to come.

Catering is a serious business. It is important to understand the cost of *not* leveraging our brands across this hidden channel. If we, as brand managers, do not to pursue catering as a business option it should be because we choose not to; not because there isn't the time, expertise or organizational skills to get it done. Otherwise it is a lost opportunity. The decision to be 'in' or 'out' of this revenue channel, must be strategically made by each of us. Period.

Taking catering seriously

My long-term vision is that all brands and multi-unit restaurant operators will eventually extend catering services through their corporately owned stores and their franchise communities. Today, in many cases, our franchise communities are further ahead in catering than that of our corporate strategies. I believe the reason for this is because "necessity is the mother of invention". And so, as franchisees struggle to build their businesses, they already know that catering can add top line sales for their stores.

The build-out of our brand catering strategies will take a natural course because it makes sense for our balance sheets. There is a revenue pool that can be considered as low-hanging fruit and we are not harvesting it properly as a community. There is an incredible amount of efficiency and growth to be realized here. Once we have the information we need to do catering well, we can mobilize our resources to aggressively pursue it.

If structured and managed properly, the catering revenue channel will bring the QSR, Fast Casual and Casual Dining segments healthy financial returns.

If we embrace this change idea as an industry and the industry takes the opportunity to build the catering revenue channel for its brands, then each of us will need to go through the exercise of layering our own look and feel to create a new brand experience.

This is where the entire magic exists and is the most compelling reason why our multi-unit restaurant operator community should enter into this revenue channel with a big commitment.

Once we complete that exercise, we will be in a perfect position to note and plan how we will integrate these business processes into our current business model. Clearly, if we can grow and develop new markets, we will all benefit in the long run with higher sales. This top-line sales growth will impact our industry right through the entire supply chain.

Adding catering to our business model requires a process of layering these new services on top of our current operations; it is scalable and the barriers to entry are low. What's more, those brands with more assets to leverage have the most to gain by considering this strategy. It's all about volume in our business. It's the only way that we can make money in our operations. Volume, volume, volume!

Once we have proven to our customers how great our catering services are for their needs, they will continue to use and recommend those services and products to their families, friends, colleagues and so on.

As we succeed in this channel by providing top-quality, high-efficiency catering experiences to our customers, we will experience the magic and synergy of the *cross-pollination* of our messaging across our catering and retail channels. The synergy will be amazing! We will discuss the best strategies for cross-pollination between our catering revenue channels and our in-store retail channel in Part Three of *Get Catering and Grow Sales!*

If we make a strategic leap to market and service this different channel for our brands, we will build excitement throughout our own organizations and in the communities that we service. The result will be an increase in our top-line sales using our existing assets. Operators will make more sales, more money and service their communities even better.

Rapid sales increase with few incremental costs

In my experience, I have found that sales will solve most business problems no matter what business you're in.

As I mention above, there is a *huge* opportunity today for our brands to see a rapid growth in sales in this segment with very little incremental cost to our current infrastructures.

The assumption is that as service providers, we can execute on these acquired sales and make our customers happy and satisfied in the process of the execution. At the same time, we need to grow these sales by operating efficiently so we can increase our gross-margin dollar contribution, which is a whole discussion on its own. This concept is not well understood yet as the flow through of catering dollars to the bottom line is substantial.

This logic is not unique to our business model. Universal business logic tells us that if we can layer incremental revenue on top of already existing assets, then we've hit a home run in our business. Horizontal and vertical growth markets have been a topic of business study for decades. Catering is a horizontal addition to our business structures, and the key to success for all of us is in understanding the impact of layering these incremental catering sales on top of our existing operations.

It is critical that we understand that we are describing a completely different business than the retail business we are already in. Everything about it is different. But this is what makes this whole potential so exciting. Because it is so different, it allows us to be able to execute these services by leveraging everything we have put in place over the last four or five decades. We have a lot of idle capacity in our ability to manufacture more goods and services out of our existing production facilities (stores).

The sales cycle and workflow for catering orders is completely different from that for executing retail operations. This difference is due to the subtleties of the transactions required to fulfill the demand for the service.

Catering is a business within a business; a business unto itself.

How do we implement the "business of catering" into our operations?

Where is all that "catering lunch money" going right now? It's going to independent shops such as Chinese food, local take-out, grocery, pizza delivery and so on. From our perspective, as a revenue channel, catering is informal and not well organized. Our messaging is unclear and our standardization as a community is not coordinated. As discussed earlier, this results in confusion both internally and externally. Ultimately, we are failing our customers and building more bad will than goodwill for our brands when we execute catering poorly.

I argue that much of that corporate money is not getting spent in our community, as it should be because we have done a poor job as a group at defining our services to this market. We have not aggressively pursued the dollars that are on the table here.

What's more, many of our potential catering customers already buy from us in our retail channels.

Just how would catering be implemented in our industry as a viable business for multi-unit restaurant operators? It is going to take a serious commitment. This opportunity is large – imagine incremental sales growth of 20 percent to 30 percent? This can be achieved largely because we are using our current assets. This is true **efficiency.** We don't have to build additional infrastructure to capture and execute these sales right out of the gate.

This integration process will not be complicated, providing we have taken take the time to clarify our strategy, and develop training, education and operational manuals. Equally as important, we need to invest in the right technology in order to scale these best practices across our entire corporate and franchised systems. All of this will need to connect to our existing IT infrastructure so that we have real-time visibility into our businesses.

We can develop this market as a community. And this would be a great collaboration in terms of making catering a standard need for our customers. If we do not create a community standard for ourselves, there is no real incentive for innovation among our community in this area of expertise. We are seriously underestimating how much money is on the table here. We just don't understand it well enough. To me, it is clear that we are under-serving our existing clients, and the opportunity to provide them more services is right in front of us.

The collective power of our multi-unit restaurant community is on a grand scale. We have the ability to influence our consumers as a group, which means more sales of products and services for everyone. This is especially exciting when, as a community, we are capturing sales from markets that are non-traditional for us.

Question: If as a community we invest in an under-serviced market together, will the top-line sales of that market grow for our group? I believe the answer is "yes". I have seen it with my own eyes on a case-by-case basis. Each time, when we see an organization make a serious commitment to catering for their brand, they succeed in growing sales quickly. But, *they decided* to do it.

I want to help you make an important connection again at this time. I am certain that you have already thought about it for your own brand.

As your current customers already buy from you and already trust your brand in terms of retail purchases, if you simply offered additional services to your established customer base, never mind pursuing new customers, because of that trust, these established customers would spend more money with you on these services.

We will become experts at showing customers that they have a need for our additional products and services, and we will meet that demand every day, because that is what we do. We are in the hospitality business and as such, we will go to great lengths to make sure our customers are happy. This is where the storytelling for our brands needs to take place. Each of us as operators needs to layer our own brand experience across the customers' expectations. We have to exceed expectations to really succeed in the long run, no matter what revenue channel we are focused on.

Customers don't know what they need and/or want until we, as operators tell them. As an industry, if we agree on standards and best practices as it relates to catering, we can mobilize our community's energy and work together to capture more sales for everyone. But, to do so, we need to create standards by which to measure ourselves properly. Over time, we can analyze this data and collectively understand and learn what needs to happen in this market from our perspective to meet the needs of our customers. After all, sales are client-driven!

To this end, we need to tell the story of catering properly both externally and internally, so we may clarify our services, and make sure that we understand the business well enough to ensure that we create a sustainable and long-term revenue channel that will actually grow our sales at a pace that we have not seen in many years. I believe that catering will grow into a channel that will be equal to the growth we experienced with drive-thru and breakfast. But, it will take time and perseverance from all of us.

Our customers spend billions and billions of dollars in our community. Because of this, if we can offer and deliver additional, positive brand-service experiences to our customers, we will simply grow our top-line sales. If we are filling the market demand and make it easy for our customers to buy from us, they will certainly spend more money with us.

There will be challenges, of course, but as we will learn through experience, adjustments can be made at the unit level to accommodate this sales growth. When that becomes our main challenge, we'll have smiles on all our faces. It's always easier to fill the demand for more sales than it is to generate more sales. Acquiring additional revenue is the hard part.

Just don't forget that in order for any brand to be successful in the catering channel, there must be strategic alignment at the executive level. There must be a vision, a business plan for the channel that must include policies, and procedures for the execution of these orders. As we continue with the idea that catering is a different business, it is crucial to leverage existing management processes on top of this business.

To acquire catering sales as we could be, we will need to duplicate our current management processes such as sales and marketing, menu development, operations, accounting, reporting and so on. These processes will need to be independently layered on top of our existing retail business, but follow our branding. It's everything we are already doing as organizations today in our retail operations with a different intention and methodology attached to the consumer offer, from messaging to execution.

Dignity and professionalism will create a solid return on investment

In *Get Catering and Grow Sales!*, I have attempted to take a logical "business theory" approach towards the task of defining what I believe has to be done for each of us to succeed in this space. My definition of "business theory" in this case, is that if it makes us money, we should do it because that's just good business.

Although a few studies have been conducted on B2B catering, at the time of writing *Get Catering and Grow Sales!* it is difficult to find any authority or accurate data on the subject. This leads me to conclude that this channel is still widely misunderstood and that the opportunity for success here cuts across all of our powerful brands. How can we know how we are doing in this segment if we are not measuring it properly? Clearly part of having dignity and professionalism in our catering business is making sure that our financial and reporting tools are in place. This requires a new perspective on our P/L's if we are to interpret our financial data properly.

The catering revenue channel, for our community, is still being defined. The data will eventually present itself as we continue to explore and make a commitment as an industry to fill and grow the demand in this segment. Saying that, we need to begin by agreeing on what our definition of this revenue channel is, so that we can track and analyze the data in the years to come. Hopefully this book will get the conversation moving. There is so much to discuss.

Our industry must document the standards, expectations, and benchmarks. We will need to measure ourselves to be able to continue to justify further investment in this model.

As a whole, the multi-unit restaurant community is under-serving the market for corporate catering. Together, if we move our efforts towards dominating that market, and extend our services to our customers where they also work and play in groups, revenues will grow for all of us.

If we are to move forward, we need to be professionals at all touch points of the catering experience for our guests. This includes a clearly communicated strategy both externally and internally and an investment into ensuring the details are executed the way we want them to be. We must also ensure strategically, that each of us remain consistent with the brand culture and experience that is unique to each of us.

As I suggested earlier, because unified standards do not currently exist, we need to invest time and energy into creating these standards, as well as education and training tools for our community. We need to invest in the right technology tools for our team members so they can manage their daily tasks while providing great service to our guests. If we do not make this investment, we will fail miserably in the long run, as it relates to succeeding in this channel. It needs to be talked about, defined and studied both in our boardrooms as well as at industry conferences. As an industry, if we are to achieve any real sense of success here we will have to take the potential seriously as it relates to building this channel. We will need to share the space.

We have a responsibility to service this channel with dignity and professionalism, so that we may reward our guests with a fantastic service experience and meet the market demand while protecting the goodwill already held towards our brands.

With more value for our customers being created through proper execution, our industry will grow its non-traditional revenues and earn profits that can be reinvested back into our brands. This is how we will provide ROI to our shareholders, by growing new sales channels.

If we do not grow these sales, someone else will, and we will have lost the opportunity to capture the market, using the power of our brands. We'll be spending all our time playing catch-up instead of leading the way, as I believe we could. It is our responsibility to take the lead here.

The business methodologies for the catering revenue channel, set out below, translate across all multi-unit food retailers, across all food categories and formats. The logic applies to QSR, Fast Casual, Casual Dining, and, one could argue, Fine Dining. The same logic also applies to the grocery industry, specifically in their deli sections.

In the past, many in the industry have attempted to launch catering strategies that have failed. Few have achieved any sense of scale in the catering revenue channel. I am certain that the reason for this is that we just have not taken the time to really understand how we can service this channel properly, without distracting ourselves from our core business.

As I mentioned earlier, today, only a handful of national operators have managed to grow a substantial catering channel across their systems.

In addition, there are many regional operators who have had fantastic successes with this channel. Over the years, these companies have blended many of the concepts that we are discussing in this book into their operations. What's more, if not for the catering revenue of these brands, they would not have been able to survive the deep recession that we have been experiencing the last several years. And now, as we come out of this sales decline, we are seeing that catering sales are in fact growing again.

Many of these successful operators understood the strategy early on, long before I came along, and then committed themselves across their whole organization to leverage their brands within the catering revenue channel. It became part of their vision and culture, just like it did at Tony's Deli.

Because of my catering operations, Tony's Deli had free cash flow of more than $1 million annually, on $2 million in annual sales. Half of those sales were catering sales.

Granted, it was only a single store of 1,700 sq. feet, and I was a hands-on owner-operator day in and day out.   However, being on the spot allowed me to control my variable costs more easily than in a multi-unit restaurant environment. What's more, I could observe what worked, what didn't and develop my systems. I suspect that as a group, we need to set our own expectations as to what our numbers should be. In any event, it's the business logic that is important here.

The same basic business principles from the deli are consistent across multi-unit restaurant operations. As these concepts are extended across our existing assets, we need to be very firm on our control process in order to provide a predictable and consistent experience for our customers at the same time ensuring that we protect our brand equity.

Given the right effort and focus in the multi-unit restaurant environment, we can layer up to $5,000 per week, Monday-to-Friday, in incremental catering sales, on top of our existing operations. Keeping in mind holidays and such, we are looking at an annualized increase of about $240,000 per year in incremental sales revenue per unit.   I used the assumption of only 48 productive catering weeks in a year.

Of course, some stores will perform better than others, depending on their locations and demographics. And for the same reasons, some stores may not do catering at all. Each of us will have a different footprint and unique situation.

One reason this amount of extra revenue is so achievable is because of the efficiency and the order sizes that catering will represent as part of the sales mix.

I have purposely left Saturdays and Sundays and holidays out of this calculation. From my perspective, if you can generate business on those days, those sales are a bonus. Saturdays were the busiest day of the week for me at Tony's Deli.

To help demonstrate what needs to happen for each of our stores to reach $1,000 per day in catering sales, we would likely need between six to eight orders per day, depending on the menu mix and our catering order averages. In some cases, we will see larger orders and may only need to execute two to three orders on those days to reach that sales goal.

Can you picture what $1,000 per day in incremental sales looks like for our operations, on a per-store basis? In Part Three I will explain my views on why catering margins should be higher than our retail margins, which further outline the profit potential.

Catering is about relationships.

Adding catering services will help our brands build more local community

Catering properly using our existing infrastructure will require some resource commitment. The resources are mostly limited to time and planning and a redefinition of some of the operations. From an equipment and/or real estate perspective it requires very little incremental cost to enter this revenue channel.

Throughout the pages ahead, I explore some of the many subtleties as to why catering out of our existing stores will help build additional goodwill in our communities, at the same time providing us with a fantastic opportunity to leverage our brand visions and messages between catering and in-store retail channels.

The catering and retail customer is often the same person. The subtlety here is that the demand driving the services for catering for this client is completely different than the demand driving in-store retail services for this client. Single consumer, different needs for different circumstances.

Remember, our customer is loyal to our brands because we are able to provide them with good value and great service. If we can leverage that brand loyalty across new services, our customers will love us for it. It makes their lives more comfortable, convenient and less stressful because it's one less decision they have to make. We need to serve them where they live, work and play, in addition to having them come visit us on occasion.

However, we must appreciate that the value propositions between these catering and retail services are completely different, and each revenue stream must be met with precision and control, using best practices as required, in each channel. We must set the standards and expectations for our customers so that they will buy more from us.

PART II – The Theory

Successful catering requires a deep commitment across your entire executive team.

Let's look at the academics

The work we have been doing at MonkeyMedia Software with multi-unit restaurant operators is specific and focused. We invest ALL of our time energy and resources towards helping our clients set the bar for their catering service expectations. Moreover, we are focused on helping with strategy as well as educating operators as to how seriously they must take themselves if they are to successfully leverage their brand across the catering revenue channel.

The adoption of the model for scaling and systematically growing this revenue channel across our entire community requires a serious paradigm shift by our multi-unit restaurant leaders.

The first step towards that shift is to recognize that catering needs to become part of our community's identity. The second step is that operators must then adopt this industry culture and make sure that it becomes part of their own company culture, so that all stakeholders are bought in.

Once that happens, we can get started, and I hope you will soon see why this is important. Read on.

First we need executive alignment followed by a thoughtful menu

Once we have executive alignment as a first step then we can begin to think about our catering menu from the very beginning of planning our catering experience. In my experience, this task is by far the most difficult one for operators to wrap their minds around. Many get stuck in the paradigm that their catering program is essentially an extension of their brand's current retail menu. This assumption can be *deadly for our brands*, and we must realize that the catering experience begins with menu development, including R&D in production methodologies, packaging and distribution methodologies.

I find this is especially true in the larger and more corporate multi-unit restaurant environments, where stores have already been "tooled up" to manufacture certain kinds of menu items for their in-store experience. Of course, we all appreciate that creating new menu items for a brand can be challenging, from concept to market testing. In addition, we also understand that layering in the manufacturing process and distribution process can be overwhelming if you have no previous experience in this channel.

From a purely academic perspective, the ideas discussed here are focused towards leveraging the power of our brands across a different revenue channel. The demand for our services in the catering revenue channel differs from the demand for our services in our other revenue channels such as take-out, delivery and in-store dining. The products and services we offer for catering can be a subset of our in-store products. The simpler we can make our catering menus, the easier it will be for all of us to scale these services across our existing physical infrastructure.

Here is where I'd like to see our community get unstuck. It is wholly possible that our current retail products should not be the same as our catering products.

As operators, it begins with a shift in the paradigm of the menu development process. While the catering experience must be consistent with the brand flavor profile and the look and feel of our brand messaging, the entire manufacturing and packaging process of these products may be a subset of our established offerings, or they may be a new offering completely.

Strategy and Dedication

My concepts start with the strategy, and this goes back to menu development. You've got to begin there and you have to be open to a shift in the paradigm. If you are not able to do it because you are not able to invest in tooling up and tweaking operations, then you might not want to get into it.

You take one company that has a brand so strong that they can decide to change how they are perceived by pulling in, say, a coffee business into their existing operations. They can do that because the brand is respected. You want to be in the coffee business? Be in the coffee business.

And you want to be in the catering business? It's the same thing. The only difference is scale. It seems easier to sell one coffee to one person than to sell 20 coffees to one client. But it's the same thing. Just requires different execution methodologies.

Often, it's just a matter of selecting a very simple menu of existing in-store products and then packaging and selling them differently. This allows us to use existing raw materials and reduces the requirement for adding new ingredients. In addition, we must allow for a differentiation in the packaging, pricing, presentation and consumption experience.

This means that our customers' catering experiences, from a menu and packaging perspective, should have a very clear differentiation from our retail service channels.

For simplicity's sake, as well as looking towards scalability, I argue that when formulating our catering menus we are far better off defining a subset of our menu offerings that can be easily executed for catering, guaranteeing a successful outcome for our customers.

Imagine rolling out a catering program with branded packaging and the right story attached to it, with products that provide for a positive on-site consumption experience!

Although some operators have a difficult time with this concept, I am seeing a trend where others are beginning to understand this viewpoint more and more.

Driving incremental sales is the ONLY reason to do catering

Remember, this effort is only worthwhile if we drive incremental sales.

Through our work at MonkeyMedia Software, we continue to see that when catering is executed properly by the brand, stores are generating up to an additional $1,000 a day for every store that does catering, for weekdays Monday through Friday. In addition if brands can build a Saturday business, consider it a bonus; our weekday business will be mostly corporately focused, whereas our weekend business will be mostly non-corporate. Note: This is a general rule and not necessarily always the case. It will depend on the market(s) our specific locations trade in.

If we take this opportunity to do the math, we begin to understand the impact that the catering revenue channel will have on our entire community. For example, if a brand has 100 stores offering catering, using the assumption above, catering can represent an additional $100,000 per day in incremental sales across the system, five days per week (We'll just leave weekends out of the equation for now). This analysis results in an additional $500,000 per week in incremental catering sales for the brand. Imagine the impact of these types of numbers on our bottom lines!

If we take the time to learn the needs of the catering market, and understand the correct pricing strategies for that market, we can decide where our brand might want to position itself in the market place. I'll remind you again here that this is about using the power of our brands to service a horizontal revenue channel.

Once we understand the demand that is driving these services, our catering sales can yield us higher margins on these incremental sales, compared with sales of our in-store retail channel. Because of the subtleties that are driving the demand for these catering services, as a community we can ask for higher menu prices from this market.

As long as we can execute a flawless catering experience for our customers, and focus on meeting the demand for what is driving these services, we will soon learn that in fact our catering sales are more profitable sales than our retail sales. As such, although catering sales may represent up to 20-30 percent of our total sales mix, it can contribute up to 40 percent of our overall gross margin dollar contribution to our bottom lines.

A visual table to help with the math

We have prepared the *conservative* table below as an illustrative example. Our check averages for catering will vary from concept to concept, however we used an average lunch price of $12.50 per person for the example below. This translates to an average order size of less than 16 people, in this example.

Should you be interested in a working version of this table, please reach out and we'll show you the math behind the math! We have used the assumption of 22 working days per month (Monday - Friday). You can see that the results are that each store needs to achieve less than three catering orders per day to generate $14.2 Million in incremental sales. I will explain more on Gross margin dollars in Part Three.

Estimated Catering Revenue Based on Industry Averages	
Check Average	$199.38
Number of Stores	100
Monthly Revenue per Store	$11,812.56
Annual Gross Catering Sales System Wide	$14,175,072.00
Operating Days per Store, per Month	22
Daily Revenue per Store	$536.93
Number of Catering Orders per Day/Store	2.693088629
System Wide Gross Margin Dollars (After RM and Paper)	$10,773,054.72

Courtesy of MonkeyMedia Software

Our goal here is to create an experience for our brands that travels well outside our four walls. The dynamics between our retail and catering service channels will continue to be very different and because the key sales drivers are different there is an opportunity to market and charge for our catering products and services differently compared with our retail restaurant services. We will discuss this in more detail in Part Three of *Get Catering and Grow Sales!*

Each of us will need to rationalize this idea, both internally and externally within our organizations, so that when our clients challenge us on our pricing strategy, we will be in a position to defend it well. The cost structure of our catering channel is different than our retail channel, as we will discuss further on. As such, we need to take a hard look at our portioning and our pricing.

I believe strongly that a well-defined catering program will complement our existing assets and make our per unit profit/loss statements very healthy. Imagine a healthier top sales line, a healthier gross margin line and happier operators. All this will pump up the volume, and, as we all know, the food business is a volume-based business. Profitability will come with more sales volume, assuming that we as a community manage our channels properly.

If, in fact, we can achieve this as a community, it will translate into a better-quality experience, lower labor costs, more purchasing power and higher profits for our operators. These profits can then be re-invested back into our community to help us grow together.

Set Expectations for Your Brand

At Tony's Deli we developed one of our best tools for leveraging the brand in our packaging. Our boxes were of high quality, and in addition to aiding with our food handling practice, it helped our customers connect with our catering service.

We displayed them prominently in the restaurant, stacked high on a shelf ready to go, so that people who entered our store would see that our catering deliveries would arrive in this beautiful packaging.

I also had a chalkboard made and wrote "Today's Deliveries" on it. Whoever opened the store that day would get the catering list and write line by line all the deliveries we were doing that day. Customers would walk into Tony's and see that we had 30 deliveries going out the back door. That created an incredible amount of buzz around our catering services!

You can set expectations for your brand. When someone orders from one well-known brand they are choosing one experience over another. From the perspective of the operator, it's a strategic decision. If you want to be in the catering business you have to define it for your brand, do it, and tool up your store to produce it. I am certain that if you layer a good catering program for your brand across 1,200 stores you've got a minimum of a $150 million revenue channel. Conservatively speaking, this represents less than $500 per day, per store in incremental catering sales.

We are seeing this, up to $1,000 per day per store, because the brand is powerful. If you take a brand that is making a billion dollars and not making money, or their margins are thin, and you add $150 million on that structure, using the conservative numbers above, you're making tons of money now.

Leveraging our brands

Leveraging brand equity is not a new idea. We have all seen multi-unit restaurant operators do this across foodservice and grocery channels for many years. One can easily find many products of highly regarded branded restaurants for sale on grocery shelves, from pies, soups, sauces, spreads and so on. Of course, as a community, we have found many ways to leverage our brands, including drive-thru, take-out, curbside and food catalogue channels.

When it comes to taking branded products to the consumer via the grocery shelves, many of us are simply licensing our brands to third-party manufacturers who may have additional capacity in their manufacturing plants. Because our community's brands are well trusted with today's consumers, when our customers are shopping in the aisles of their local grocery stores they appreciate finding those products that they can take home. That emotional response is part of our consumers' ongoing relationship with our brands.

Although licensing the manufacturing of our branded products to third-party manufacturers will provide us with another revenue stream, it is just one more way to leverage our brands.

In the case of the catering channel, it is very different from a simple license agreement with a third-party manufacturer; because we are not going to outsource the manufacturing of our catering orders to a third party.

One might argue here that as we roll this strategy out to our franchisees and licensees, they can be considered as third-party manufacturers of catering, however, as franchisors, we will have a responsibility to set up our franchise community for success in the catering revenue channel.

As brand parents, we need to control the catering experience at the unit level in order to ensure long-term success with our brand loyalists.

Leveraging brands as it relates to driving catering sales is, however, relatively immature in the North American marketplace. I am clear that there is a profound lack of understanding of how the dynamics of this channel can work for the multi-unit restaurant operator.

The demand for catering services is driven differently compared with those for our retail channels. For these reasons, and probably a few others, growing catering sales for our brands and unit operators continues to be very confusing for our community. The end result is that as a group, we are confusing our consumers as well and actually diluting our brand equity due to poor execution.

The entire language and conversation, as it relates to fulfilling catering transactions, differs from our retail transactions. Moreover, the entire business logic of catering and the order workflow is radically different from what we are already doing in our retail operations.

To add even more complexity to the equation, the very same customer who is in our stores to buy their favorite lunch, now wants to place a catering lunch order for 50 people for next Thursday, and they want it delivered to their office.

This type of customer request is tough to handle operationally if our strategic plan and our systems are not set up properly. The energy that we must extend at the unit level to take that order and execute against it is not only inefficient, it is *dangerous for our brands* because of the many things that can go wrong if our plan and systems are not in place. There can be a high risk on a catering transaction that our customers will not get the experience that is consistent with the brand. As such, we need to focus on setting the right expectations from the beginning of the service process.

If our catering products and services are not professionally rolled out in our community with agreed upon standards and procedures, catering will actually dilute our brands' value, as there will be a disconnect from the retail brand experience our customers have learned to trust and expect.

As multi-unit restaurant operators, we have invested billions of dollars into getting our consumers to trust our brands and we have spent considerable effort to create a predictable, positive experience in our in-store, retail sales channel. All of our assets are already deployed, and our operations are moving along with some efficiency and repetition, although, as always, there is room for improvement. As a community, we have shared our knowledge and created conferences and trade shows to continue our collective learning. Over many decades we have created an incredible amount of infrastructure to service our retail customers. Our brand loyalists have come to love us for it.

All of a sudden, many in our community go down the path of catering without a proper strategic plan or proper enterprise systems. Those in our community that do so are risking everything that we as a group have worked hard for. All of the billions of dollars and all our energy that we have spent over the years towards growing and nurturing our brands are put at risk for these reasons.

I urge our community here to stop and imagine how the catering channel would work for each of our brands. Why does catering make sense for our financial statements, assuming we use the current infrastructure of our community to deliver services to the catering revenue channel? What makes the catering revenue channel so academically sound, from a pure business perspective? At the same time, what are the risks that we must mitigate to protect the brand? What about order entry? What about food handling? What about...?

One reason that this business channel is so academically sound is that as operators we can leverage our brand equity across our already-committed customer base. When offering catering products and services to our existing customers, we are nurturing our customer relationships further, actually developing even more loyalty to our brands if we execute properly on our service commitment.

By catering in a professional manner, the message we are providing to our customers is that we have another service to offer, should they have the demand. By doing a better job at defining this market segment, we are letting our customers know that we are willing and ready to help them with their catering needs, and that we have taken the time and energy to create a positive, consistent and high-value experience for them. When our community can clearly define that message for our customers we will be rewarded both financially and with more consumer loyalty.

Depending on our store demographics each of our retail customers has a need, or knows someone who has a need for feeding groups of people. The circumstances for feeding these groups will vary by occasion, however, the core transaction workflow process and business logic will be consistent.

Catering and delivery is a business that must be thoughtfully formulated, so that we can service our customers with the same level of quality and service that they have come to expect from our brands. We must further leverage and protect our brands properly by not providing poor experiences in service and product. Each of us has a fiduciary duty to protect our brands at all costs. There is far too much at stake here for all of us.

Saying that, it is critical that we continue to appreciate that the subtleties of executing this catering channel are completely different from those of executing our retail channel. This means that we will have to provide our organizations with the proper expertise, education and tools to make sure that our catering customers are serviced to the high standards that we set in our strategic plans.

By the sheer power of our community's brands, we will attract incremental sales in catering once we begin telling the story properly of how our multi-unit restaurant community has become experts at providing a flawless catering experience.

As I have stated over and over, we *must* develop a deep appreciation that the service methodologies and the dynamics of the sales, order entry, production and delivery transaction for catering, are radically different than what we have in place for our existing retail operations. Once we have a clear understanding of this fundamental difference, and we believe that the power of our brands can attract incremental catering sales, we are ready to take the next steps.

Pulling our teams together

We must work hard to align our executive teams, our management teams and finally our entire organizations. Once we are each aligned internally, and we are committed to a strategy, our customers will certainly follow.

If there is any doubt from our executive teams about the catering channel, *we must agree not to move forward.* This alignment work is the most important – and perhaps the most difficult – that our community will have to do to ensure success in growing, managing, and maintaining a worthwhile catering revenue channel.

Once we have achieved this level of understanding, if best practices are then established, implemented and followed, and a serious and professional commitment is made to this channel for our brands, we will quickly learn that the magic behind what makes catering so profitable is that we can leverage all of our existing assets, systems and people across this service channel.

There will be very few incremental costs associated with growing catering sales. We will have a few key requirements, mainly in terms of filling positions such as order takers, delivery drivers and other minor catering-related expenses, but overall we will find that entering into the catering revenue stream does not require a lot of capital or any additional infrastructure.

Because there are low barriers to entry into this market, if we deploy our assets and get the message out properly, we will see a rapid increase in sales.

Assuming our operators have planned well and support their vision with the appropriate resources of strategy alignment, education, training and technology, our bottom lines will improve dramatically as we increase sales in this channel at the unit level.

Failure to do this properly will lead to operational inefficiencies that will hinder our ability to execute, and that will result in dilution of our brand. Cross-pollination of messaging and marketing for our consumers between our catering and retail channel becomes a very important part of the shifting dynamic that needs to be managed by our existing operations.

We'll chat more in Part Three about how to manage the dynamic of competing resources that will begin to take shape in our organizations as our catering sales grow on top of our existing infrastructure.

There is a big opportunity for those that want to seize it!

Because many members of our community have been ignoring the catering stream as an incremental revenue channel, there will be more for those of us that decide to take on catering as a serious business.

What I find most interesting when visiting the boardrooms of the nation's multi-unit restaurant operators is that when talking to them about catering there is a profound lack of strategic alignment and direction. I have thought long and hard about this challenge. The paradigm shift has not been made yet.

As retail revenues continue to be squeezed by more competition and over-saturated markets, and our consumers continue to have more services to select from, we will see the paradigm shift.

As brand parents, we have a responsibility to consider every possibility that exists where the brand can be leveraged to generate new and incremental revenues. And as business people, we know opportunities are plentiful, and for the really big brands, their phones ring off the hook with vendors trying to give them ideas of how to make more sales or more profits. There continues to be a lot of noise around 'squeezing costs' and trends such as online ordering and social networking. I truly believe that the answer to saving our community's slower growth is right in front of us.

Because of our community's lack of experience in developing and growing this catering revenue channel, some multi-unit restaurant operators believe that it might not be part of their core competency and as such, catering might take them away from their main focus as a business.

In my opinion, this conclusion has not been well thought out. Any multi-unit operator who thinks catering should not be part of his/her core business should really take a hard look at the details. *Catering can be worked into the plan. What's more, it absolutely should be worked into the plan.* We just need to take the time to understand the opportunity and the cost associated with not looking at the catering revenue channel as an extension of services.

There is considerable demand for feeding people in groups in the corporate world. Corporations have constant meetings, presentations, celebrations and educational seminars and are driving the demand for these services. This market has always been there, and it will continue to grow as corporations continue to try to find methods of getting their people to work longer hours and attend training and education seminars. Feeding employees is a good way to get them to show up for meetings.

In each instance, the guest eating our food is part of a gathering of individuals who have a very short window of opportunity to be fed on any given day, based on a packed business agenda. Often, the demand for catering services can be over several days, or it can be several meal parts on any given day. The key to success in this channel is to be able to create an experience that allows the customer to feed their guests quickly so they can go back to their meetings. Time is money in the corporate world, as we can all appreciate.

As mentioned earlier, many multi-unit restaurant operators get hung up on being able to offer a predictable service experience for their brand in the catering channel using their current in-store retail menu.

Remember, the subtleties and order dynamics of catering are different. As such, the menu offerings in our catering channels must be different, and can be (and should be) at higher price points. In addition to this, portion sizes can be reconsidered as part of our menu development process. We will discuss the opportunity for portion adjustments later on in more detail. Suffice it to say that if we do a great job at differentiating our service, we will have no problem getting higher price points, especially if we "kill them with service!"

It is our responsibility to provide our customers with a quality experience that they have come to appreciate from our brands. If we do so, we will see our incremental catering revenue soar rapidly.

Many operators will continue to think of catering as an "add-on" business. As such, they will fail miserably trying to execute these services. For those operators that decide to do it right, there will be more profit to be made.

Growing catering sales will create wealth for our community

Every successful brand in our multi-unit restaurant community began with an entrepreneur with vision and passion. This same entrepreneurial spirit will also build catering into a successful revenue channel for multi-unit restaurant operations within our existing infrastructure. This entrepreneurship is not only a great thing, but it is the cornerstone of our success as an industry and further what brought us here in the first place.

Many of us have built massive brands from that entrepreneurial passion, have done a fantastic job of telling the history of the brand, and have been very successful at preserving the culture and vision of the brand's founders.

Catering will be new and exciting for all of us. It can serve as a force of revival for our organizations. In today's environment, it is difficult to grow same-store sales by trying to drive more store traffic. Because of this, employees can have a hard time feeling motivated and excited to do the same thing day in and day out. They are tired of not creating the growth in revenues that they can feel good about. After all, our people who work on our frontlines work hard for our customers. As such, it can become frustrating for our people if quarter after quarter there is only a slight increase or even worse, a decline in same-period sales. It presents a difficult challenge to keep our people motivated when there is little to get excited about.

Catering is something our organizations can get excited about because *it can grow*. Stakeholders in any organization always feel more excited to be part of a growing experience.

When we at MonkeyMedia Software work with multi-unit restaurant operators, and we see their plans come together and their commitment to catering takes shape, it quickly becomes one of the most exciting topics of conversation in the organization. Leveraging the catering channel will infuse an entrepreneurial spirit into our organizations that will invigorate and excite all of our existing stakeholders, including shareholders, executives, managers and our frontline workers.

If, as multi-unit restaurant operators, we successfully layer our catering order execution on top of our existing operations and supply great catering products and services, we will also create excitement amongst existing and new customers. This will keep our customers coming back for even more services.

This excitement leads to customers becoming even bigger brand ambassadors. This idea is very powerful, because it allows us to build on the relationships we already have with our customers.

I'll go one step further to say that if we execute catering properly for our customers, she or he will come off as a hero to their colleagues, friends and families – the people they have had the responsibility of feeding. This result will build even more goodwill with our customers and increase the opportunity for loyalty to our brands, through their extended network. As a brand, we just made everyone feel great! We made our customers heroes!

When guests eat food at a gathering and they are enjoying the consumption experience, they always ask: "Where is this from? It's delicious!" When that individual has that positive catering brand experience, it will crossover to them becoming a fan of that brand. As operators, we now have created a fantastic opportunity to cross-sell our retail services to that same person. I refer to this phenomenon as cross-pollination between our services. It's a fantastic opportunity that we will discuss in Part Three.

Once we get going on this channel, each revenue stream will feed the other. The caveat here is that we **must** execute a positive and predictable experience every time. We can only do that with a strategy, commitment, training and education, good people, and by putting the right tools in place for our people to execute their jobs against our strategy. This requires investment.

Leveraging assets is simply smart business. But we still need to invest!

It does not matter what business we are in, but if we can achieve incremental sales growth, using existing asset infrastructure we have a formula for economic success.

This is the key economic element that makes it all work for our multi-unit restaurant operators. So much has already been invested in current assets at the unit level. There is already activity in the store, customers coming and going, equipment running and employees trained in the culture of our organization. Transactions are flowing at the retail end, and for the most part, all of our systems are in place with a successful working model. As a community, we are generating revenues already, and the basic business challenge is how to increase sales at the unit level.

We will only be successful in leveraging these assets if we make the right investments into our products, sales, marketing, and operations for execution. We must clearly communicate our aims and intentions to stakeholders within our organization as it relates to catering: What we are trying to achieve and how we are going to get there by using everything inside the four walls of our existing facilities.

Remember, catering is a different business and the entire order-to-cash cycle is different, as is the production and packaging of the food, all the way through to the distribution of the orders.

Once the order arrives at its destination, there are many decisions that we can make for our brands that can help each of us to differentiate our catering service in the marketplace we compete in. We will find that the consumption dynamics of our guests are completely different, and all parts of the experience need to be well thought through, designed, rolled out, managed and measured.

I caution readers here: as our incremental catering sales begin to grow on top of our existing assets, we will begin to see a competition for resources at the unit level. This can be overcome with good planning, strong operational instructions, and with an investment in training and systems.

If our catering sales grow even more, we will then need to do the hard work of redesigning our future facilities.

Over a typical business day, the execution of catering in the new setup would work out well for the unit manager because the delivery of our catering products need to leave the building long before our retail breakfast, lunch or dinner rush begins. This is one of the beautiful things about layering catering on top of our existing revenue channel, by the time we are ready to handle our in-store customers, catering is already out the door!

If we make the right commitment, we will have succeeded in layering incremental, higher-margin sales across our existing assets. The contribution to our bottom line will be substantial. In addition, if we successfully grow incremental catering sales across as many of the existing assets as possible, we will have also increased the equity of our brand due to the increase in our cash flow and profits.

Catering will positively affect your bottom line.

Catering just makes sense at the unit level

Increasing store traffic these days is not only difficult but it is variable, depending on seasonality, weather, and the general economic conditions that we are all facing. Anything we can do as a community to increase sales will certainly have a positive contribution to the overall gross dollar margin at the unit level.

Another reason why catering makes sense for our community and all our brands at this time is that because we are under-serving the market, the only way we can grow is up!

As I mentioned earlier, if catering is executed properly and best practices are implemented, the impact on gross margin dollars will be substantial. It is not unreasonable to expect an additional $1,000 per day, Monday – Friday, per store in incremental catering revenue. If we implement the right catering menu and we understand what the market can bear in terms of prices (and portion sizes), we find that even though catering may only represent up to 20 percent of our overall system sales, it can contribute up to 40 percent of our gross dollar margins across the system. I appreciate that I have commented on this earlier in *Get Catering and Grow Sales!* However, this is the most crucial aspect we need to understand as operators. The financial impact of this channel on our community is worth billions and billions of dollars.

This high-margin contribution is only possible because of the premium that we can charge for executing these services properly for the corporate community. There is a premium that customers are willing to pay if they believe that their catering experience with our brand will be a stress-free experience.

For many owners operating on the margins of financial stability, catering can present itself as a fantastic turnaround strategy, and if we drive these sales and execute the service properly we will have a major impact on the bottom line of our units. This logic extends itself to both the corporate and franchised systems.

Catering is not an add-on business; it is a business unto its own.

Our unique complexity as multi-unit restaurant operators

I have come to learn that the complexity of the environment of a multi-unit restaurant operator is unique. Being a retailer, driving store traffic is not only difficult, but it requires a constant commitment to marketing, advertising and in most cases couponing. Social networking is a new frontier that is also being explored in our community.

It is uniquely complex for an operator to create a brand experience that is consistent across markets, not to mention to put in place all of the details that need to be thought about to make sure our guests leave our brand experience happy.

As the number of our units grow, so too does our complexity in operations, reporting and systems. If we continue to build these business processes on poorly executed business logic, we are simply layering inefficiency into the system, which will ultimately cut into our margins and profitability. If our management is not tight enough, we begin to see diminishing returns as we open additional units. We will only be able to grow to certain levels as operators, and we have an obligation to all our stakeholders to be the best that we can be through all services that we offer.

Franchising adds even more complexity and dynamics

If we are a franchisor, the business model becomes even more complex, as we become the service provider to the franchisee. In a franchisor-franchisee relationship, the franchisees will always want new ideas, support for trying new things, and they will want to appreciate what it is that we are doing for the franchise fees they pay us.

As the franchisor, we will be focused on growing more franchises, which in itself is leveraging the brand. However, our existing franchisee community will be fighting for the survival of their own locations. Offering catering as a revenue channel to this franchise community is required. These franchisees need our franchisors to help them with their execution. We have to provide the leadership necessary for the franchisee to be able to execute catering the way we want so that it services the customer and ultimately protects our brand.

Each of our franchisees will need to go through a "catering education" program and as the franchisor; our focus needs to be on helping them drive more catering sales at the unit level.

As franchisors, we can provide a "catering certification" process for each franchisee that wants to provide catering services as part of the overall brand experience in their communities.

If, as a franchisor, we do not formalize and support a corporately structured catering program, our franchisees will go off and do catering their own way. It will be another lost opportunity for our brands, the franchisee, and the customer. It will eventually erode the goodwill that we are trying to create within our franchise community as well as with the guests of our brands.

As we mature our retail-based businesses and saturate most major urban markets with our brands, competitors begin to fill in the gaps and draw on our customer base. Our organizations get pulled in many directions, and in a worst-case scenario franchisees begin infighting and disagreeing on the corporate strategy, and on occasion the franchisee's business begins to fail. When that happens, they fight hard for survival and in that process, the franchisor begins to lose control over the brand experience and specifically that operator, as the operator is simply just doing what is required to stay alive so they don't lose their livelihood and their investment into their franchise.

Each retail unit represents a potential profit center and each unit represents an opportunity to build brand awareness and create goodwill for the brand in that community. As such, catering once again rises to the surface as a potential revenue channel that should be defined by the brand, and the franchisor can look towards this channel as a turnaround opportunity for failing locations.

Again, if catering is in our strategy, as the brand managers we must define the experience, create the instruction manuals and support the effort with systems. One might argue that all the systems we have in place for duplicating our retail experience from market to market also needs to be done for catering. It requires its own set of planning, sales strategies, marketing strategies, operational strategies, menus, policies, and procedures and, of course, the technology to control and scale the whole experience for successful execution.

Technology options – our community is overwhelmed!

The technology available to multi-unit restaurant operators is abundant. Making the right choices is critical for long-term growth and sustainability. And the technology required to execute a sizeable catering operation might not lie in our existing technology portfolios. We see many operators use online ordering technology or try to drive their catering orders through their Point of Sale (POS) systems for execution.

These technology strategies are incorrect because these technologies were never architecturally designed to handle the workflow and/or dynamics and subtleties of the catering revenue channel, from the perspective of how to execute the services. Catering requires a constant commitment to business-to-business selling, conversational ordering, invoicing, managing of accounts receivable and many other subtle dynamics that today's POS systems and online ordering systems cannot help with. It is less about technology, and more about the business logic of catering. We have to do it "right" on paper first, before we can even consider technology.

One of the most important decisions we need to make for our brand, if we are going to pursue this revenue channel, is which software system to implement. It is essential that the system(s) we select is specifically designed for the execution of the catering order transaction type.

It is *not about online ordering* and it never will be. The online world is simply a window or shopping experience for our customer. The shopping experience that customers have online with our brands, should take them through a service experience that is relevant to the type of transaction.

For example, they may want a take-out order. Clearly, take-out orders should be sent to our existing POS assets for order execution. That's what POS systems are built to do. In the case of catering, sending an online order to a POS system is the wrong strategy. The POS asset is not designed to handle any of the ordering dynamics of a catering order.

There is specialty software available today in our community that can handle our catering transactions and the right enterprise packages will send us the data we need on the schedule we want with some programming and workflow design.

One of the biggest traps I see out there for all our major brands is that many of them adopted online ordering in its early stages. So, they do get online catering orders, but that's where they get stuck. No systems for execution of the orders are formalized or in place, and so as they try to scale catering they simply fail at the execution because they are using inadequate tools.

As such, the lack of a catering strategy as part of our brands' core business strategy creates internal tension from the lack of controls and predictability. Mistakes happen and customers get frustrated. In a multi-unit restaurant environment we need to have a repeatable, predictable and quality experience, every time. Otherwise, we will dilute our brands' experience.

Catering is basic business

How can I say that catering is "basic business" given its complexity? I say that it's basic in that it is as simple as providing a new service to our customer. We take an order, we manufacture the food, we package the food and then we either prepare it for delivery or for pickup, depending on the client's requests and the parameters we put around our delivery and pickup policies and procedures.

As operators and managers we must constantly be considering our shareholders and maximize the profits of our organizations. As a fundamental business argument, growing incremental catering revenue, providing that we communicate the vision and leadership to do so, is simply basic and good business practice.

As discussed in our earlier example, as an owner-operator of 100 stores, we should be thinking about raising our incremental daily sales by $100,000 per day from Monday - Friday. Using that logic represents a potential incremental annual sales increase of $24 million for the brand, in this example. If we consider that the margins of catering can be as high as 40 percent, we are looking at a highly profitable model for our multi-unit restaurant community. This makes sense from an abstract perspective. It will not happen without the commitment and investment by our operators and the coming together of our community to finally take this channel seriously for ourselves. We need to spend time together at driving this business as a group. This will result in sales growth for our entire community.

Getting there will take gumption and belief in these fundamental concepts.

What's happening with catering in our multi-unit restaurant community?

If we study the marketplace we will find at the national level that there are only a handful of chains that have created any sense of scale in their catering operations. Although there are many regional and independent operators that are experiencing great success with layering catering into their businesses, we have learned that the larger the operator, the more challenging it is to scale the experience across the brand.

For the purposes of this part of our conversation, I want to focus on our big national brands. This is a sweet spot from my perspective and I believe that these larger operators are having a very hard time understanding the impact of this channel within their operations. As we travel to these operators, we see many brands in test markets and we see some brands that have extended their catering sales by over $100 million per year. For these operators, catering is a serious business.

I have thought long and hard about what it is that allows these few brands to succeed in this selling space.

How are they able to do it? What are they doing that the other national brands are not? To me, the answer is clear and simple; it's always been about the strategy of deciding to be in the business or not. Too many brands have attempted and failed at catering in the past and because of that they are gun shy to try it again. They feel like they have made too many false starts and that catering "doesn't work" for their brand.

I argue that catering doesn't work for them because they have not considered it properly. They do not have the in-house expertise or the intellectual property that is required to be successful in this channel, and this is something that they have to make a decision to invest in.

There are many catering career-oriented individuals who understand the dynamics of this business, and they have been successfully involved in growing sales for other brands within this channel. I'd recommend that we start by hiring a business leader with a vision for growing this revenue channel. Saying that, it begins at the top the organization. Catering has to become part of our brands' overall business strategy and not just looked upon as "add-on sales".

PART III – Let's go deeper into Get Catering and Grow Sales!

Increase your catering sales by

$1000 per day, per store.

Make room for catering! Here is where we will discuss how to layer a scalable catering revenue channel for our brands into our existing infrastructure. However, Just before we get to it, I'd like to set out one simple but big idea on the table.

Retail dollar out of manufacturing rents

Because catering sales can represent up to $1,000 per day, Monday – Friday, in incremental sales for the right stores, the economics of those locations will change. Moving forward with the idea of catering in mind, in some cases, one might consider establishing new locations outside of downtown urban centers but with a focus on delivering to the businesses located downtown.

With proper strategic planning and the right facility footprint, we can think about how we might set up catering-specific stores in certain markets, particularly those markets where there is density, such as in any major metropolitan city. In some of these circumstances, there are opportunities to leverage our brands in these markets by executing catering out of a commissary-based environment. Although this model is different from the model of doing catering out of each store, there is some efficiency that we can gain by centralizing the production and distribution of catering orders to our customers.

Part of the magic at Tony's Deli was that our retail store was off the beaten track, yet we were close enough that we could deliver catering to Vancouver's downtown core within five to eight minutes. The rent was great and we were yielding a retail dollar out of a space where we were paying lower commercial rates, instead of high retail store rates. This resulted in a lower-cost structure that increased our bottom line.

This strategy is easier to execute for corporately owned stores than it is in franchised systems, however there are franchisees in our community that themselves are multi-unit restaurant operators. When developing our strategies for catering, we should consider this model where it might make sense to do so.

I will not discuss this concept further in *Get Catering and Grow Sales!* as I am planning to follow this book up with a more in depth look at the pros and cons of this model. It will be part of my future catering discussion series. You will find a list of future topics at the end of the book.

So, with that in mind, let's begin the process of diving deeper into the steps and concepts that we as a community must take in order to be successful in our catering revenue channel.

I will switch from speaking from the perspective of "we" at this time to the perspective of "you". My reasoning here is that although the steps and concepts are global across all our brands, each of us will need to adapt our own variation of these ideas. Ok. Let's get to it.

What is your catering strategy?

Document your strategy

Let's get into a step-by-step view of where and how you need to start this planning, rollout and execution process.

Here is an approach that I'd recommend for any brand that wants to build out a catering strategy: Your strategy will depend heavily on the current overarching structure of your organization. Your strategy will be impacted through the relationships that you have with your franchisee and licensee communities, as well as the structure of how many corporate stores you have throughout your system. In fact, as each of you has a different structure, you may even have to develop a strategy for each part of your organizational structure. So, the plan for doing catering out of your corporate stores may in fact be different than the expectations that you will need to set at the franchisee and licensee level. We will discuss more of these ideas later on.

Let's continue to break it down further. The plan:

Focus your executive team on providing a logical business plan for your catering revenue channel. During this planning phase, you must identify all of the resources you will require including the organizational structure that you think you will need to execute a catering program across the brand. As you go through this high-level process, do not worry about the business issues or the costs associated with these resources. This is a "just get out of the box" kind of exercise. It is worth noting that you can always hire an external facilitator for this kind of exercise.

As your vision comes together from a qualitative perspective, begin to look at the numbers. What will it cost to generate $1,000 per day, Monday – Friday, per store in incremental catering sales across the brand? As we continue on in Part Three in *Get Catering and Grow Sales!* we will dive deeper into how you're going to methodically grow your sales to reach these targets.

You will learn through this process that because catering is driven by a different set of consumer demands your products can be tailored and packaged accordingly, to meet your consumers' needs. Because of this fantastic opportunity, this allows you to consider different products at higher price points than what you may be doing in your retail environments. In addition, as you look further you will see that because of the market conditions for these services and depending on the experience you provide for your customers, you can charge a "premium" for your services. This will result in yielding you higher margins on your catering sales than you may be getting from your retail sales. (This is a BIG idea that I want you to hold onto throughout the rest of *Get Catering and Grow Sales!*)

As we go through the math together, you can see that applying this business logic will help define why incremental catering sales at higher margins will become such an important business for all of us. The key here, and why catering is so profitable for us as operators, is because as an operator you are driving those sales on top of existing assets. Your operations will flourish and experience stellar sales growth and a much healthier bottom line once this is established.

Create an enforceable policy-and-procedure manual for catering

I find from time to time that before operators go through the planning and strategic alignment process, many brands want to test the waters. They put up a few signs in the stores that say 'we cater' and they wait to see what happens.

Not only is this approach risky for the brand, but it can potentially create bad will among your customers and your employees because they will fail at the execution of the catering services as they lack direction and structure from management. There is often a lack of leadership in these instances. It's a mess, more often than not.

Because of the power of your particular brand in your markets, you can move forward with confidence in your community as it relates to catering. Your customers will call you if you offer them alternative services, as long as you provide them with a predictable experience every time. And did I mention quality? Do I need to? You are in the food business. Quality is a given.

Once your strategy is agreed upon and the plan is laid out, hold off on any in-store marketing until you have solidified a policy-and-procedure manual for best practice catering execution.

These policies and procedures are not something you need to invent. There are catering-centric professionals in the industry that can help you with this important task. As part of your resource planning, you will require catering leadership and that person must take on the responsibility of documenting, training and mobilizing your workforce to achieve the success we are discussing here. As a side note, the right software system and technology can play the role of "enforcer", as the intellectual property captured in a good software package will have many of those policies and procedures already built-in for the users of the software to leverage.

Even with great software, you will still require internal training materials for your organization's catering operations. These materials need to be documented properly so that you may educate your team on what the vision is for your catering service as well as communicate to them the best practice that you want enforced for high customer satisfaction. Without the right strategy and education, great software will not get used the way it was intended.

Develop marketing materials that are catering specific

This basic concept is not any different than what you are already doing for your retail sales channel. Taking this approach is consistent with my earlier perspective that "catering is a different business" and not just an add-on business. As such, you will need to be able to tell your "catering story" properly, and set client expectations. You will need to educate your customers that in fact your catering experience may differ from your retail experience and you need to tell them the reasons why this might be the case.

In order to really drive incremental, higher-margin catering sales, you are going to have to make a lot of noise around it, both internally and externally to your organization. One advantage you have as a multi-unit restaurant operator is that you already have real estate, people, and, most importantly, customers.

As you develop your marketing materials for your catering channel, think about your in-store opportunity first. You must make your catering services VERY visible to your in-store guests. *A word of caution here; your in-store guest may very well be your catering guest*. Because of this, if you do not direct and handle catering service inquiries properly you will not only confuse your customers, but you will upset them in the process.

The messaging for your catering services must be well defined and you must use your store for marketing these services. This will help to build awareness with your customers.

Use your wall space, tabletops and your menu boards. Find a new area in your store where you can post "today's deliveries." Make a list of all the names of the organizations that are using your catering services each day. Make that list visible to all and you will see how inquisitive your current in-store customers will be by knowing businesses in your market that are using your brand for these services. At Tony's Deli, we had a large branded chalkboard on the wall and we hand wrote all of our deliveries on that board each day. It only took five minutes and we made it part of the store procedures. Some days, as we executed 40 or more orders, we actually ran out of room on the board. However, the impact on the awareness about our catering services increased rapidly among our in-store customers. It created a lot of excitement in the store!

Once you nail down your in-store marketing program for catering, you have begun the cross-pollination process of educating your current customers about these additional services.

Now that we have discussed a little bit about cross-pollinating your catering messaging at the store, I want to discuss the single most important marketing asset that is available to your organization. The most valuable marketing tool available to you as an operator is internal to your organization. Catering NEEDS to become part of your language and your culture. You must train your people at the operations level in all aspects of "telling your catering story" to the public. They should be able to direct inquiries to the right individuals, as well as make sure the customer is aware that your catering business has its own unique set of policies and procedures that, as an organization, will provide the best possible catering experience to your customers.

You will need to educate your frontline people to speak the language of catering and make sure they are trained well enough to direct the customer to the right person for perfect service execution.

Your catering dedicated people will need a tool that they can use to take the order and communicate all the details of those orders to the kitchen and the drivers. When a customer places a catering order, the order dynamic is conversational. Therefore, as your catering customer service representative is taking your catering customer through the ordering process, you must provide for the proper tools for them to do so.

As I stated earlier, I see operators trying to execute catering with their existing POS assets. It just doesn't work as the order flow and execution dynamics are completely different for the catering transaction then they are for the retail transaction. Towards the end of this section I will discuss how technology can interact with your catering and retail channels.

OK. Now that you have nailed down your in-store marketing, and you have trained your valuable people properly, you are now ready to move on to the part of your marketing program that needs to be externally focused. Your catering story can be told using all your preferred methods of advertising in which you have all become experts. *One note of caution here, <u>DO NOT</u> use discounting or couponing to incentivize your customers to use your catering services. Just do a good job, and they will always come back because of the relationship they already have with your brand.*

Successful catering is a team effort.

Hire the right catering sales staff

Hire the right sales people to knock on doors and work the telephones. Remember, in this sales channel you are cultivating relationships with people; however you are often providing services to the corporations they work at. Pursuing sales needs to happen at the community level, as well as at a national level, if you are a national brand.

You will need to have skills on your team to carry out direct selling to corporate accounts, cruise ships, bus tours and the general corporate delivery segment – anywhere that could use catering services. In this mix you will also get the opportunity to cater private parties, graduations and other types of large gatherings, however, your bread-and-butter business will be corporate delivery.

As your sales team hits the street they will learn that catering purchasing patterns can be negotiated well in advance and contracts are available for larger accounts. In addition, as the process of driving catering sales is a business-to-business transaction, you will need a resource that is focused on selling to the corporate community in the markets in which you want to build catering sales. Relationship-based selling is required to succeed in the long run.

Extending catering to the franchised and licensed communities

This is a critical topic for discussion in our community. As a corporate operator, if you have not figured out the model for catering in your own stores, how can you extend these services to your franchised and licensed groups?

Many brand owners tell me that their franchise communities' are screaming for a unified catering strategy for their brand. They are hungry for leadership, ideas and systems. In today's economic climate, many franchisees are not waiting around for head office to provide them with these catering strategies. As such, what we are witnessing as an industry is a disconnected experience that is not consistent across our brands. As I referenced earlier in our conversation, this type of behavior can be very dangerous for any brand and for the relationships our brand owners have with their franchisees.

I am absolutely certain that in order for franchisors to keep their franchisees happy, they must be able to help them grow their top-line sales. It's why franchisees bought the franchise in the first place. They purchased the intellectual property rights that our brands have developed over many years, for a specific territory. As a result, a franchisee looks to its franchisor to help them grow their businesses.

As we extend catering services to our franchisee and licensee communities, we must recognize that there is another dynamic being introduced into an already complex mix of services. A franchisee is also our customer, but the customer that the franchisee is ultimately servicing is loyal to the brand, and belongs to the brand.

It is our responsibility as franchisors to service our franchisees and make it as easy as we possibly can for them to own, operate and grow their units.

As we further consider the challenges related to growing catering sales for our franchise communities, we will need to spend some time understanding and discussing which services need to be centralized versus decentralized to the franchisees. Remember, as the brand parent, we need to control as much of the brand experience as we can. I believe that doing so is in the best interest of all stakeholders all the way through the service chain.

The consequences of not pursuing this will result in franchise communities that will begin doing what they think is right for their individual franchises without consideration for the brand. This is especially true if the franchisees' units are not performing well. It can turn into a blame game that can damage the brand, and ultimately result in customer attrition.

I would like to see a strong debate about this topic in our community; a debate that leads to solutions. In the work we are doing at MonkeyMedia Software, we are well focused on extending the right tools through all the franchise communities in order to maximize the catering opportunity.

Positive co-existence between the franchisor and the franchisee is essential. The franchisee community is already facing so many challenges in growing their businesses that any franchisor that decides to invest in growing the catering revenue channel for both their corporate and franchised stores will leapfrog those who decide not to.

I believe that the best strategy for multi-unit franchisors is to centralize services where possible in the catering revenue channel; sales, marketing, call center management and order management, payment processing and accounts receivable management. In addition, IT services need to be considered for the catering revenue channel.

If, as franchisors, you can provide these services, then you will have succeeded in providing a single point of contact for your brand's catering customers. This is very important for the psychology of your customers because the demand that is driving catering is different than the in-store demand for retail services. As such, the experience is different. In catering, your customers need to be handled consistently with established, predictable, high-quality service. If you provide centralized customer service functions, you will be able to train customer service experts who are specifically designated to maintaining the customer relationship for your brands. Although it certainly crosses over into your retail channel, for catering it is essential. The art of this will depend on your ability to make sure that your customers feel like they are interacting on a local level. This can be put in place with some great training.

Another benefit to centralizing these services is that your franchisees can simply focus on order execution and not on getting bogged down in the administrative process of managing catering order dynamics. Imagine a store that only has to worry about getting orders out the door through manufacturing and distribution of the catering experience. The rest of the issues can be taken care of for them, resulting in less pressure at the store level.

As a selling point to your franchise communities, you can suggest that your responsibility to them is to grow sales, provide marketing and customer service. If you do that well you will then set the franchisee up for success in the brand's catering program.

If this is handled properly at the brand level it will really take the heat off at the unit level, where franchisees are just trying to keep up with their retail businesses. Once you layer catering sales on top of your retail channel, you will begin to see that these two revenue channels begin to compete for resources at the unit level.

From the retail customer's experience, there is nothing worse than watching a server answer a catering phone call while they are waiting in line to place their order. It is critical that you focus on the customer at all times. And so, if you centralize some services, you will have happier franchisees, happier customers and most importantly an efficient service process where both the retail and catering channels can provide the best possible brand experience for the customer.

There is more to talk about here related to growing catering sales in the franchise model, however, your corporately-owned stores must have their catering business in order first.

Growing catering is a GREAT business decision!

Now that we have gone through some of the analysis that needs to be done at the brand level, and you see that the goals you have set out above are achievable, you understand that success in this channel will have a HUGE impact on your profit and loss statements and cash flow at the unit level.

As you deploy your existing assets, and generate a new revenue stream by simply creating the right customer experience for your brand, then it becomes obvious to see that leveraging your brand across this channel is just simply a great business decision.

The proposition of a catering business for your brand is low risk and requires more psychological change than it does asset change. There is a three-step process that can be followed towards success:

1. Strategy

2. Education

3. Technology (software)

It will become all about defining what catering means to your organization and then layering the right processes internally for execution. That will put you in a position to ramp up sales!

Some core functional areas of a multi-unit catering operation

Let's build out the functional tasks that need to happen every day to make your customers happy while maintaining your brand experience. I will begin with a discussion around the selling process.

As an operator, you need to understand what you are selling when it comes to the catering channel. Yes, of course the food taste, quality and packaging are important, but it's not what you are selling! So, what is it that you are selling when it comes to your catering revenue opportunities? I will answer that question shortly.

How to get catering sales

For many multi-unit restaurant operators, the idea of having a sales team and pounding the streets and knocking on doors is daunting. You must recognize that to service the catering channel properly, you need to get very good at business-to-business selling. To drive sales in the catering revenue channel, you will need to build relationships within your communities' corporate sector. The audience for your catering channel exists in the communities in which people live, work, and play. It's the same community of people all the time doing different things at different times. Your job is to create an experience that appeals to them for each occasion.

Although the catering relationship for your brand is with the customers who favor your brand, the catering transaction itself is with a corporation when servicing the corporate market. To acquire and maintain these relationships, you will need an ongoing sales effort to these corporations in your communities. This is especially true at the national account level, which can become a very important part of your catering sales success.

A necessary component of any successful catering operation is a focused and direct business-to-business sales effort. There is a traditional B2B selling methodology that you will need to adapt including outbound telemarketing as well as site visits. Your catering sales team will have the sole purpose of developing and driving new relationships. The question of outsourcing these services – or not – will become clearer once the different models that can be applied to the sales methodology are better understood. Each of you will have a different set of circumstances.

When it comes to all of the successful operators we work with at MonkeyMedia Software in the catering revenue channel, each of them have made a commitment to a Director of Catering leadership position. Depending on the size of the organization, we often see catering sales managers working under the Director of Catering. This will vary from organization to organization, but the concepts and functions put forward here apply to all sized companies.

The psychology of the catering sale

Now that you have someone who is thinking about growing catering sales for your brand, let's discuss what is driving the demand for these catering transactions. Depending on your catering menu mix, 85 percent of your business will likely be corporate meetings and 15 percent will be for personal gatherings. You can develop different menus, for different catering segments, but as you layer this on, your operations will increase in complexity. As such, you need to move forward with care and understand that each time you add a layer of service you increase the risk for your brand. We will discuss more about menu development later on. Thinking about the 85 percent for the moment, let's focus on the key demands for these services.

Every single day, in every single city in North America and probably the developed world, people are having meetings, celebrations, seminars and many other types of gatherings.

The buyer of your catering services and products is the person who is paying you for these services. In many cases, it will be a company. However, keep in mind that the company that is making the purchase is NOT your customer. Your customer is the person within that organization who is tasked with calling your brand and placing the order on behalf of the corporate entity that they work for.

In order to understand the psychology of that sale, you must first understand the dynamics the person placing the order is facing inside his or her organization. Why are they calling for your catering services and what are they hoping to solve? What is the value proposition for them personally?

You must keep in mind that the person placing the order is the same person who will take the heat internally if the order is messed up either in quality, timeliness and overall customer experience. There is often a high fear factor for this person and what is driving the demand for this order is the *stress* associated with not getting it right. The decision of what brand to order from today may or may not be up to the order placer, but they are accountable internally for making sure the execution is flawless.

Here is a typical office lunch catering scenario:

The executives have meetings all day tomorrow with important prospects. The meetings were organized at the last minute and they've got a 45-minute break at noon.

As soon as those executives exit the meeting the food must be there and ready for consumption. If there are any special dietary requirements, the order better be accurate because if the critical details are missed, the order placer (your customer) will take the heat for getting the order wrong.

The number one factor that you need to solve for, from a psychological perspective, is that you need to acquire and maintain the order-placer's trust. In addition, you will need to ensure that the consumption experience is right or you will not only lose the trust of the order placer, but also all those who are consuming the catering experience.

Here is where the theme of cross-pollination appears again. If you do it right, you can not only gain new catering customers from the people consuming the food, but they may also transfer their personal purchasing to your retail channel because of the positive brand experience they had from your catering services. Of course, like any transaction in the food business, you will only be as good as your last meal served.

To succeed in growing your sales for this business channel, you will need to follow best practices and execute what you know well. After each catering order is executed, you need to ensure that the proper systems are in place to ensure that you do the proper follow up and ask for more business.

Herein lies the psychology of the sale. The people who need to place catering orders want to have a relationship. Like all relationships, you have to have a base of trust and understanding. You must always put the customer first and acknowledge and validate their experience. If they have a negative experience, it is your responsibility to make it right for the guest and turn it back into a selling opportunity. And so the catering wheel continues to turn.

One concept that I would like to introduce to you at this juncture is what I refer to as "brand rotation".

As discussed earlier, breakfasts, lunches and snacks are being eaten in offices, every day, in every single city. Most of the time, there is a *catering list* that the customer will use to place orders, and they may or may not have negotiated agreements. Your sole objective is to be on this list. Once you are successful at doing so, you need to make sure to just focus on the things that you do well.

As you continue down the catering revenue stream, you need to be cautious. Not only will your customers call for a catering experience, but at the same time they will also try to add a take-out order into the mix. This is where you need to understand the subtleties of what lies beneath the conversations at the ordering level.

As operators you need to take on the responsibility to define the lines between your businesses and train your people to be able to direct the inquiries into the right places. The opportunity for cross-pollination of the brand between the retail and catering markets is powerful, but each experience is very distinct in terms of what the conversation is about at the service level.

When speaking with your customers, you need to ask the right questions. "Would you like a catering experience or would you like a take-out experience?" Of course, as a brand you can provide both of those services to your consumers, but I do not recommend that you do so on the same transaction or check.

If you delve deeper, and your sense of definition is completely clear in terms of what type of transaction goes where inside your organization, then you can create the architecture to help support all of the policies, procedures and systems that will follow your business strategy and sales channels. The successful implementation of these policies and procedures will help to create the sales volume you will need to make it all work well for your customers, and ultimately for your operations. You must take time to define the transaction types and invest heavily in training your people with what to say, when to say it, and where to direct the customer for the best possible brand experience.

To conclude this topic, I hope that you just hold onto the idea that the catering transaction is a *stress-driven transaction*. This means that the person on the other end of the phone, e-mail, fax or online order needs to be made to feel relaxed. The requirement for building catering sales transactions is to reduce that stress. To build that type of sales culture for your brand, will require the right person. That person needs to be empowered by the strategy, plan and resources that the leadership team has agreed to.

The sales methodology for growing more catering revenue

When discussing the sales methodology for catering, keep in mind that the formula is basic and simple, and does not need to be overcomplicated at any point in the process. Before any salesperson can begin going out to market, they have to have good products and services they can believe in.

The methodology begins with qualifying the lead for catering. You must become an expert at identifying leads that are qualified catering buyers - identify who those people are, people who would be likely purchasers of catering services. Find out about them and how big their opportunity is for your brand.

Once you have the prospect in your database, you can now begin the selling campaign. The campaign steps are simple:

- Call by telephone to introduce your brand's catering services.

- Arrange for a time to deliver a free promotional sampling from your menu. This promotional package should be consistent and predictable every time. Everyone gets the same thing.

- Give the sampling a name such as 'The Gourmet Food Platter for Five.'

- Make sure all packaging and marketing materials are included when delivering the package.

- Have promotional food delivered at off-peak hours. After all, you are giving it away. No sense competing with real dollars available at breakfast, lunch or any other day-part that you might be considering for catering.

- Follow up... Follow up... Follow up.

- Stay on them with both task-based follow-ups as well as keep them on your marketing campaign.

That's it. That's the whole methodology. You are in the food business. You generate sales by feeding people. Sampling sells in our business. All it takes to get a good customer in this business is a positive, predictable and consistent experience that meets their needs. If you execute the promotional basket well, you will see a quick return on the investment and the phone will ring at the next opportunity.

Catering is smart business.

What are you actually selling?

You are selling an experience. Catering is simply another revenue stream for your brand, not unlike take-out, delivery or drive-thru.

You have to meet the market demand while doing this, so first you have to solve the customer's problem, and it begins by satisfying the fear factor on their side. The administrative assistant who is under the gun needs to have a stress-free experience with your brand. Through successful execution to the boardroom table, you are selling an experience that fulfills the demand of this particular market.

Allow me to really drive this point home. Of course the consumption experience has to be great, but what you are really selling is peace of mind for the customer who is ultimately responsible for getting the food to their internal guests.

Your brand represents greatness, trust and pride. You are selling the entire culture of your company. You need to create a parallel universe in catering as you have already done with your retail revenue stream(s). The experience needs to be consistent with your brand because what you are actually trying to do is leverage all of the brand's goodwill as well as existing infrastructure and assets.

Growing catering revenue requires business-to-business selling

To be successful in growing sales in this market, you will have to consider yourself as an expert in B2B selling. In order to be an expert, you will have to make sure that you tell your market that you are an expert. This means that you have to behave as such and understand that you are trading in a corporate environment. This requires attention to how you conduct outbound calls and onsite presentations.

Then, as you drive your frontline resources to sell catering in-store, you can begin to really focus your efforts on direct-selling campaigns to organizations within your community. You can ask for their business via telephone, e-mail, direct mail, social networking and Internet based advertising. For bigger brands, television and radio can also be considered towards building awareness of these services.

Of course, this is all just lead-generation work, and there are many external resources available for you to generate even more leads. Prior to hiring your sales team, I would recommend that you invest in maximizing the use of your four walls first.

Given that you will be mostly focused on a B2B market, when the inquiries come in the expectations and stakes are high. Two very high priorities for this market are time and money. At the initial contact point for your catering services, the information that you provide has to be clear, concise and fast. Your catering customers are very busy and placing an order is only one of hundreds of tasks they have to accomplish that particular day. Everyone in the corporate world is under deadlines.

As a service provider, somebody needs to be on that telephone representing your brand, and they need to be trained well so that they can provide a catering experience that is consistent with your vision and core values. Each operator will have a different take on what that needs to look like, however, what is important here is that you have to take the time to define your desired outcome.

Remember that your sales grow only if your execution is as good as it can be. So if you are failing on the back end, the whole front end will fall apart too. And it will happen quickly.

That's the negative side of not getting it right.

Relationship selling needs to be part of your core strategy

Because you're selling an experience to your customers to reduce their stress in this channel, you must also continue to appreciate that your customers are also having an intimate experience with your brand outside of your four walls. Your customers will be eating your food, and in the catering market, because you are feeding larger groups of people outside of your four walls, the relationship you have to build with your customers will be the key to your success.

It would be wise for you to assign catering customers to an account manager internally so that you can look after them properly. Every issue needs to be followed up on and every customer is important.

And if anything goes wrong in this relationship, you need someone internally who can call the customer quickly and make it right. By doing so, it will help to maintain brand integrity and show the customer that you stand behind your brand. This behavior creates a bridge of understanding and keeps the customers coming back.

As an operator, you don't want to be struck off their internal catering list, so to be effective, you must keep track of your customers and keep reaching out to them with exceptional customer service.

Let's discuss menus for growing catering sales

There is a lot to say about menus as it relates to catering. From a higher level, if you agree with the perspective that catering is its own business that needs to become part of your core business strategy, then allow me to point out that, in fact, catering needs its own products and packaging. There are many qualified organizations that can help your brand with this challenge. Most likely you have current relationships established that can help you as it relates to product development.

You don't have to get stuck in the idea that your catering menu has be exactly the same as your in-store menu.

You can even create signature-catering products that are only available in catering. If the customer is craving that item at retail, you can apologize and explain to them why you only offer it to your catering clients. This is how you can leverage your menus to provide a different experience for your customers that will keep them coming back for more services.

The discussion about menus at this stage of our community's catering lifecycle is a big paradigm shift that our industry needs to think about. Don't worry that you may have to tool up 2,000 locations if you have different products for catering. There are ways of handling this by looking at different catering models. Each of us will have different circumstances to manage, and catering does not have to be executed out of every store.

It is not about anything else except creating a menu experience that your customers want in order to fill the demand. Much of the menu management that I am discussing here can simply be solved with different packaging.

Some of your current retail menu items may not travel well, or they may be difficult to manufacture in large quantities. Your catering revenues will live or die by your ability to manage your menus across your current infrastructure. Keep it simple and basic.

If you leave with only one single idea from this conversation, remember to simplify. Your catering business should be short and sweet in terms of what is on offer and should play a complimentary role to your take-out and dine-in business.

For each product on your menu you should know how easy or difficult it is to make, how it looks in the packaging, how it travels in the truck, and what happens to it if it sits for some time on the boardroom table. Also, you must study it from the customer's experience, to make sure that every detail has been attended to and anticipated for them to have a fantastic catering experience. All the details are important to the experience, even down to whether or not it is easy for them to find more salt. This is especially important in this channel because the consumption experience happens outside of your four walls. That changes the whole dynamic.

Order execution is the key to growing catering sales!

With catering you take your brand experience to the customer at their site of choice.

Once you have earned your customers' trust enough for them to give your catering services a try, it is show time. The order execution for a delivery at 12:15 p.m. for 100 people is completely different than serving 100 people in your take-out and dine-in operations.

There are many subtleties you will have to manage. The catering business is as dynamic as any other type of revenue stream. No two days are identical, and it is never static.

Proper execution for catering transactions requires advance planning and leadership at the unit level for proper execution.

Order accuracy – getting the transaction the way the customer orders it – is probably our single biggest challenge as a community when we discuss catering execution. There are many details to look at and get right from a production and distribution perspective. There are a lot of transition points in the lifecycle of the transaction where the order can go wrong. The big challenge in this channel is that because much of the transaction happens off site, it is not easy to turn back after things have gone wrong on the delivery or even once the customer has picked up their catering order at our stores.

For proper execution you will need to follow best practices of a catering business, some of which are mentioned in this book. In layering those functions on top of your existing assets, you will be able to cross-train your people between your retail and catering revenue channels and therefore make better use of their time.

For example, on the evening shift, the catering lead supervisor can prepare the beverages and paper service for the catering orders for the following day.

For the proper execution of $1,000 per day, Monday – Friday, per store, you will need an earlier start to the day from your kitchens' perspective. Much of your lunch business will have to be out the door by 11:15 a.m., if you are to successfully get your deliveries out on time.

Here's another example of how catering impacts your organization: It complements your existing assets, because once you have executed against breakfast or lunch for catering, your rush for breakfast or lunch at retail is still 30 minutes away. There is a lag time because of the distribution issues of catering orders.

Part of the order execution is making sure you have the checks and balances in place to ensure a positive experience for your customers.

Follow-up and dialogue become very important to the customer. As a professional service provider you need to ensure total customer satisfaction. This will yield long-term customer relationships, which is a key metric to growing sales. You have to keep them coming back again and again.

I have been trying to bring to your attention the complexity of strategically moving forward with your brand in the catering channel. You should find comfort to know there are other brands in our community that are implementing some of these strategies – and they are having success. Their catering revenues are growing and they are experiencing positive results. What should give us even more confidence is that even though the economy has continued to be sluggish, many brands are seeing fast growth in their catering channel.

As an industry, if we get it right then this catering channel will grow for many years to come for each one of us that decides to make catering part of our core business strategy.

Is your catering experience predictable and scalable?

Creating a reliable, predictable and scalable catering experience

You must keep these objectives in mind at all times when developing this channel: Reliability, predictability and scalability.

Because of the complexity of the existing tangled web of systems and infrastructure that operators have been building on over the last 40 or 50 years, layering in a new service channel is not simple. It requires thought, decision and precision. What we are after here at the brand level is simply to create a reliable, predictable and scalable service experience for this service channel.

You cannot create this experience without making the paradigm shift of menu development and planning, focused resources that are trained with precision so that the customer experience is predictable and consistently good in food quality, service and timeliness. In addition, you must methodically nurture your customer relationships in order to make sure that you, in fact, have solved for their challenge of stress reduction during the catering transaction. If you can deliver on reliability and predictability then scalability becomes a question of the right systems and proper rollout, both of which most of us need help with.

Achieving these three things means you will impact your unit-level profits like never seen before. If the implementation of catering for established brands is well handled, the market will compensate you greatly for your efforts. But you have to not only set the standards, you have to meet and exceed them.

The fact that these standards remain underdeveloped in our industry is both our community challenge and our opportunity. This, of course, is one of my reasons for writing *Get Catering and Grow Sales!*

Pharmaceutical reps – a special relationship

To be successful in this market, you must carve out special services for pharmaceutical representatives. They need to be handled differently.

The pharmaceutical industry is deeply invested in research and development. And so, in order for them to take their drugs to market, they need to educate healthcare workers on the benefits and side effects of their new medicines.

Their target audience is the doctors who prescribe these medicines. The challenge for the pharmaceutical representatives is that it is very difficult to get busy doctors to attend seminars and presentations at the best of times.

It has become standard procedure for pharmaceutical representatives to feed their audience in the hopes that they will show up for the presentation and stay there to hear their sales pitch. And so, it is very common for these representatives to schedule their presentations during breakfast or lunch.

Typically, these pharmaceutical industry representatives are looking for a high-quality experience to attract the doctors and so they may have larger budgets than other catering clients that you may pursue in the corporate sector. Again, this will vary from market to market.

As you grow a catering business, you should have a sales and service person dedicated to the pharmaceutical industry. Their network is small, and if you do a decent job for them, they will refer a lot of business towards your brand.

Depending on the territory that the representative has to service, they are often feeding larger groups of people and so their average order size can be substantially greater than other clients.

As brand ambassadors there are many opportunities for you to negotiate catering contracts directly with pharmaceutical companies, and they, in turn, can push your brand and menus out to their sales teams either regionally, or even nationally, if you have the ability to provide them with the coverage they require.

The promo package: sampling sells catering!

Being in the food business, the best way to sell your products is to provide samplers to those you are trying to sell to. We all know that promotion through tasting sells in our line of work.

Your sampler offering needs to be a fixed package. The experience of offering this sampler package should be consistent, each and every time. The objective of your sales effort is not to buy your prospects breakfast, lunch or dinner. It is simply to introduce them to your services and products, and to leave them wanting more. If you do a good job at packaging your sampler package, you will get your prospects to think of your brand the next time they need these services. Hopefully when that happens, you will have become experts at taking your catering orders and the service machine you've created will take over and ensure a positive experience for the customer.

Often I see operators allowing their sales team permission to provide any or all menu items and then simply charge the whole order off to a "promotional offer". In my opinion, this is not the right way to go about it because the idea is to leave the customer wanting more.

If done properly, you will deliver these sampler packages at off-peak hours. The last thing you want to do is mess up a real order from an established client because you have a drop-off promotional basket scheduled simultaneously.

Therefore, you must establish policies and procedures for your sales team to follow. Promotional orders should always be scheduled around your main meal times and the package you send should be standardized. There should be enough variety of products so your prospects get a decent sampling of your various offerings.

One very important point: you must make sure that you have provided all of your sales and marketing materials at the time of the promotional drop off. To facilitate success you can find a method by which the production and distribution of your promotional packages are rolled into your regular catering processes. The care you take in the execution of promotional orders will enforce the positive experience you are working so hard to achieve.

Cold calling to build catering sales

Cold calling is old school and in the case of selling catering services it works! Lead generation and market awareness can seriously be impacted in a positive way if you have a powerful brand. If, as an operator, you have more than 100 units, you can consider outsourcing cold calling services to a lead generation company. You require this scale to make it cost effective.

Outbound telemarketing can fill the corporate funnel by hitting the phones and sending information on while building product awareness. In addition, by working the phones, you are able to ask qualifying questions and fill the funnel even more for your sales team. Remember, growing catering sales is all about leveraging the power of the brand. Relentless phone work will yield sales results.

Traditional advertising – how to use it to grow catering sales

If you have a successful brand, then you know all the traditional avenues in advertising that can be used. We as a community have become experts at using advertising as a way to get our messages out there.

If we all started to do radio and billboard advertising, directed at the catering market, I believe we will see the top-line sales of our industry grow.

Walk-in catering sales – how do you handle the customer?

You will have to make a decision on how to handle catering walk-in sales at the store level. Walk-in catering sales can be very disruptive to your existing retail operations and can overwhelm your frontline people on the floor. This is especially true if the timing of the walk-in is during a peak retail period.

When a catering customer walks in and wants to place an order for catering, your retail resources will have to take their eyes off the ball at the retail store, creating a lot of risk for both the catering and the retail customer.

I believe the best model is to direct your customers to a catering specialist who is a trained expert and will be able to handle them with care and accuracy. Remember, as I have stated earlier your catering business is different than your retail business and as such, as each one grows there will be some competition for internal resources. There is a big opportunity for both internal and external confusion if your internal resources are pulled in different directions at this stage, so following strict guidelines and practices is paramount.

By re-directing walk-in catering sales to a single point of contact, you raise the service bar substantially and you will have a much better chance at providing a predictable, consistent and scalable catering process.

From an efficiency standpoint, your customers will feel well looked after if, as a buyer, they can pick up the telephone at the store and call the customer service agent directly for placing an order. The customer service agents will be well trained, and they will be in a better position to look after the customer than the store operator. In addition, there are technology opportunities to consider for online orders and for catering kiosks at the store.

In addition, if you consider this as a working model, you remove the heat from the store level and as such, the stores can simply concentrate on getting today's catering orders out the door without getting bogged down on the administrative duties of taking a catering order.

Telephone work – be relentless and watch catering sales soar!

We discussed lead generation earlier on. This section is focused on the telephone work that needs to be done on your existing customer database, which is different than the telephone work that needs to be done when you are prospecting for new customers.

Mining your customer data gives you a reason to call them. This is about rewarding those customers who are coming in regularly and reaching out to those who have disappeared. For example, it is important to reach out to a customer who hasn't ordered from your brand in the last 90 days. You need to find out why and whether or not they had a bad experience or they have moved on to another company.

If the catering contact at your client company has moved on, you should find out who the new person is. You must offer a promotional package to this new person and re-establish the sales cycle. In addition, you can now go call your previous contact at their new job with the aim of getting them on your list as well. And so you can see how the cycle continues.

I cannot say enough about the positive benefits of this ongoing and relentless effort. Keeping on top of these changes and other details is the grunt work that will keep your customers coming back for more services. The telephone remains a very important tool for your brand and you should not be afraid to use it. Use it to speak to the community, tell them what's new and thank them for their business. Use the telephone to feed them data on their ordering patterns and provide them with gifts for their loyalty.

Referrals are the most powerful tool you have for growing catering sales

Word of mouth is key to acquiring new catering sales. It is simple to acquire referrals and is very effective when prospecting for new customers. Yet, few organizations do it very well.

As you expand your catering operations across your brand and you become an expert service provider, you will soon learn that success in this revenue channel is brought by close customer contact and by making sure you are listening to what your customers have to say.

As part of the standard service process, a follow-up call should be made for every catering order that has been delivered. The goal of this call is to thank your client for their business and to find out if there are any hidden issues that need to get addressed.

If the customer is satisfied with the service level they have received, you can take the next step and ask for referrals. Once received, it needs to be followed up on.

The referral business is key to helping grow your catering services across your brand. It is critical to understand that asking for and receiving referrals is more of an art than a science and it needs to be handled with care.

If the referral turns into a relationship, you MUST take the time to thank your original customer and give them some kind of referral compensation for the business they have sent your way so that they will be encouraged to let others know how great your brand is. This is another opportunity for cross-pollinating your overall services.

You can compensate them with a small gift card for your retail services that in turn will drive more traffic to your stores, continuing the cycle. Remember, people usually don't eat alone and so if you give away a gift card, chances are that customer will bring someone with them. And that person might need catering next week! It's a win-win for everyone.

Mobilizing your most important resources – your frontline people

Enrolling your Front-Counter Resources: to me this is by far your largest sales force. If you can mobilize your people to provide leads you will seriously drive catering sales. In an organization of 20,000 employees imagine how much energy that brand can create! These are the people who work in your stores every day and who are the first to meet and serve your customers. If you look at your community as a whole, and you train them in the language of catering, imagine the impact that will have on your top-line sales growth!

Enrolling your front-counter people into telling the catering story for your brand as they are providing a retail transaction experience is probably one of the most important and high-value adjustments you can make in your organization. As customers who come in through your doors are getting looked after in the service channel they came in for, think about the selling opportunities you have! At the same time you are taking care of their current needs, you are selling new and alternative services to them. Saying that, your front counter "pitch" has to be thought about and developed. Then it has to be instilled in your people through an investment in training.

By providing the right marketing materials within your four walls and your external perimeter, you will support your people with a new catering language in tandem with their enthusiasm for your catering services. Menus should be easily accessible and catering pick-up locations inside your stores should be clearly marked and visible. With improved signage, your customers will be unable to miss that you now have new and exciting services available to them.

The key thing to remember is that if your front-counter resources are engaged in active selling, you will most definitely increase catering sales. It is imperative to create a compensation program for your people for gathering leads this way.

We trained our people at Tony's Deli to talk to our customers when bussing tables. We'd have a series of qualifying questions that our people would ask on the floor, and if the customer fit the profile our busboy got a business card and told them he'd have our sales team follow up on the conversation. After the conversation, the card was handed off to sales for execution. Our busboy was given $2 each time. In those days, he'd make an extra $12-$20 in cash during some shifts. Our sales team was so good, that our conversion rate was close to 100 percent using that methodology. Now that is good targeting!

Whatever you do, you should not let your front-counter people run with the catering ball. Instead let them gather names of potential catering clients and pass it off to the correct part of your catering team who will become specialists in handling guests' catering needs.

Get business cards – lots of them!

Getting our front-counter people to ask for business cards was a big step for us at Tony's Deli. It is difficult for many people to ask for things when they are out of their comfort zone. Part of our ongoing training was to teach our people how to look for catering opportunities. They were taught to understand the characteristics of what a catering customer might look like; and we then targeted them with conversation and service.

We paid our front-counter people bonuses for acquiring the business cards of well qualified catering leads. We had them wear buttons on their uniform that said "if we did not ask you about catering today, then your lunch is on us!"

It's what we did with the cards once we had them that became the selling experience at Tony's Deli.

If you are serious about being in the catering business you must remember that it needs to become part of your entire business culture, or you will have a hard time growing catering sales. You need to get excited about it and celebrate it both internally and externally in order to be effective.

Recognizing the different characteristics of a potential catering order

Let's discuss breakfast, lunch and dinner. Each of these dayparts will be a big part of your corporate catering business. To be competitive your menu mix will require that you sell your products by platters, box lunches or buffets. You will have to decide on a menu that works for your brand. You may even offer cocktail platters for evening parties. Each of these types of catering transactions has its own unique set of order characteristics.

To me, this is very simple.

If you have a brand that has customers, you can really simplify your menu. You may only offer two platters and one buffet as your catering products. The dynamic of a group meal, offsite from your restaurant, differs greatly from the dynamics of your clients getting in their cars and traveling to your restaurant as a group for a meal together.

There are three order types that you will need to define well for your customers, so that you can service them properly:

Group orders – the lunchroom table

This type of order can have several scenarios.

The most complex scenario is when you have a single person who is organizing a meal that is to be delivered on a specific day, and individual participants are responsible for selecting their own items and charging the purchases to their individual credit cards. To be truthful, this is a large take-out order, however, defining it as a catering order type can be very beneficial internally for your execution because the administrative and production aspect of this kind of order can be very complex.

The other scenario here is when you have the same order dynamic, but one person or entity is settling the bill.

Group orders – the boardroom table

This is probably the most common type of order for corporate catering. The dynamic here is that there might be ongoing meetings, with short lunch breaks in-between. In this type of scenario the company (or single individual) is the buyer.

As part of the responsibilities of an administrative assistant at the client's company, it is his/her job to make sure the meals are scheduled and delivered on time. In addition, it is expected that the order placer will likely have some special dietary requests. Being in this business, you need to go out of your way to provide for special requests. It's a big part of what gets them coming back for more.

To appeal to this market the catering transaction order-to-cash cycle needs to be efficient. It needs to be seamless.

Once the customer places their order what happens is up to you. How you execute these orders will matter to your long-term success as a multi-unit restaurant operator.

Group orders – training seminars and tours

Training seminars and tours are boxed-lunch and platter-based businesses. If you are going to be servicing these businesses regularly, then you need to set up your production facilities to execute large volumes and order sizes. It makes no sense to take a boxed-lunch order for five people.

For the boxed-lunch business market you should focus on a 100-box minimum. The reasons for this are clear: the process of manufacturing and assembling boxed-lunches is time consuming and difficult to execute in small quantities. You should not be afraid to make a minimum requirement for these types of menu items.

Your powerful brand can negotiate for big contracts to win this business. Focus on cruise ships, big tours and cross-country and national training seminars. There are many opportunities to provide boxed meals to hundreds of guests on a single order. At the regional level, focus on government training seminars and any administrative councils where large groups of people are gathering.

Markets for this type of service include universities, government agencies and the film and travel industry. When considering boxed meals, only provide them when the volume warrants it. Otherwise, you should focus on making your production process simpler by offering platters and trays and buffets.

Great customer service will grow catering sales!

As with your current retail business, customer service for the catering revenue channel will have to be the best that you can make it. You must set standards across all aspects of your team and you will have to invest in their skills.

You will have to teach them how you want the channel managed and executed and you will need to be consistent with your expectations for your team as to how you want things communicated and problems resolved.

The expression "the customer is always right" holds especially true in the catering revenue channel.

I point this out so emphatically in order to avoid several potential failure points, especially in the execution of the catering revenue channel once the order is taken and you are going down the production and distribution path.

You will succeed based on how well you mitigate these points of failure. This requires a deep understanding of the business logic and the workflow for dealing with problems properly when things go wrong. And believe me, things will go wrong in your catering operations every day. Investing in systems and people to drive and manage this very valuable channel for your brand will help you have visibility into your operations so that when the order does go wrong, you can make it right as quickly as possible.

I really cannot say enough about service. It doesn't matter what business you are in, if you provide the best service possible, and always smile and do what you can to make it right, your customers will always return. You need to have scripted and detailed procedures to make sure that each customer is made to feel good about using your services and ensure that you have done everything you can to get your customers to come back.

One other thing about customer service is that if you track your service issues and report them internally your service will improve.

Here are some ideas for streamlining your service methodology when it comes to increasing your catering sales:

- Reduce administrative points of contact and make it easier on your operations by centralizing incoming calls. This allows your customer service representatives to become specialists at order entry. In addition, by centralizing your order entry, you will mitigate the opportunities for errors and raise the probability of providing a more consistent and positive experience to your guest.

- When taking an order, bring up the client's record and track all discussions and transactions. If they want to place an order, take it. If they want something else, answer their question or find someone who can.

- Once an order has been keyed into a system, make sure your customer service representatives read the order back to the customer. You want to make sure your people pay close attention to the date, the time and the details of the ordered menu items.

- Teach your customer service representatives to sell properly. Overselling or underselling at the order entry point can result in a disaster for your brand experience. The guest is calling you because they already trust your brand, so at the order entry point, the person representing your brand can make or break the catering experience.

- Guests always want good value for the money that they are spending and they want a high-quality experience. It is critical to teach your frontline order entry people about your menu fully so they can recommend the right portions specific to the function where the food will be consumed.

- After reading back and confirming the order, <u>ALWAYS</u> thank your customers for calling and let them know that your company representatives are available to help them further should they need any more information or if they need to call back and make any adjustments to their order.

- ALWAYS let the customer hang up first.

Do you want to make your

catering clients look great?

Who are your clients and what do they look like?

At this point in time, it is worth reiterating that it is critically important for you to fully understand who your clients are. Your clients are people, not demographics. Their "need to feed" crosses all aspects of their lives including personal fulfillment, in the workplace, where they volunteer, where they go to school, when they gather with friends and family and so on. Their food consumption decisions are made at different times for different needs.

Now, you have your own brand vision, look and feel and taste profile. It is your job to appeal to your clients based on their food consumption decisions in order to strengthen your relationships so that they spend more money with you.

You also must remember that your employees are your customers as well as your vendor community. You need to market to them too.

Make sure your organization is clear about who the customer is in the case of each individual catering order.

The person whose head is on the block if things go wrong is your client for that transaction. Also, the people consuming your food are your clients as are your internal customers, your employees that are making it all happen. You must do everything in your power to make sure that your customers come off looking like superstars.

If you manage to create a positive experience here, not only will you have strengthened your existing relationships, you will also have managed to increase the goodwill for your brand. And if you cross-pollinate your marketing and messaging properly, you will now have had an opportunity to introduce new guests to the concept of visiting your in-store experience when they are making that specific decision.

Relationships are very important in this catering business

You are now in the business-to-business selling cycle, and you are accessing potential in-store customers in their places of business. They are your biggest ally (or naysayer) depending on the results and experience you provide.

As you invest in these relationships the success you have in catering will stand out. You must be diligent in keeping your clients close, and you must do everything in your power to not only keep them informed as to the services you offer, but you must also follow best practices as it relates to customer relationship management. Good old-fashioned customer service!

Your catering relationship with your customers goes beyond being face-to-face or phone-to-phone with them. It includes ongoing data analysis as to their purchasing habits so you can understand them better as well as always doing the right thing for the customer. You must be extremely diligent in the follow-up, and if faced with negative reviews, you must go out of your way to make sure you not only document the issue but make sure that the correct person in your organization makes it right for the customer.

Every order carried out should be followed up by a phone call to inquire if everything went as expected, and, at the same time, if the experience has been positive. If your clients rave about your service, you should record it on their file. The client should also be asked for a referral and testimonial that you can share internally and externally. These steps should be part of a scripted service process.

Logging problems so that you can make it right!

When problems arise from catering orders, it is critical that you take the time to log the issue against the customer's account.

Try these steps:

- Listen to the customer without interruption.

- Acknowledge that they have been heard and make sure you repeat the concern back to them accurately and confirm with the guest.

- Thank them for taking the time to call. Make sure you apologize to the client and let them know that you will be pursuing the issue internally and that they should expect a follow up call shortly.

- Take the time to write it up internally and make sure the right person/ people in your organization are notified and are assigned a follow-up task concerning the client to make it right for them.

- Call the client back once you are certain that the situation has been resolved in order to confirm that they will come back for more business. Record the results in their file.

Order entry is the frontline when it comes to catering

The order entry process is grossly misunderstood in our community. The order entry experience is one of the single most important parts of the catering order-to-cash cycle.

This is the first point of contact for your catering transactions and this is where the customer experiences the service level of your brand. You MUST greet them with a SMILE! This is also the place where the client is reaching out to your brand for help with this stress-driven catering transaction in order to fulfill their needs.

Working with multi-unit operators, I often find this is a major point of confusion and internal debate. Many operators have set themselves up to take orders at the store level only.

While this can be one strategy, you must consider the impact on your system's operations by taking this path. It can be done right, however, you will have to understand the impact of teaching hundreds in your organization to take orders. My perspective on this is that I believe that the distributed order entry process at the store level makes it more difficult for your unit operators to properly execute and maintain a proper and predictable catering experience.

For example, if you have 100 stores and you allow for catering orders to be placed at the store level, you may find training more than 100 order takers not only a challenging task, but wrought with risk for your brand. Furthermore, you will require more than one order taker per store, and as such, the results can be disastrous. To be successful in the world of conversational ordering, it might be a better strategy to create a role for internal (or outsourced) specialists depending on the size and scope of your organization.

There is a strong argument to be made that training specialists to be responsible for catering orders and for maintaining and building customer relationships over the phone will yield higher order averages, more accuracy and a better service experience for your brand.

Many operators I speak to get confused on this issue. The key issue here is that in our minds, we must separate out the "selling process of catering" from the "service process of catering." *Selling* your catering services needs to be done at the neighborhood level so that you can reach out and touch your customers. *Serving* your customers' needs to be approached with what is most efficient and profitable which is in the best interest of your customers (both internal and external).

When I refer to a centralized point of contact for order entry, I believe it can be implemented in various forms, depending on the structure of your organization. There is a discussion to be had around centralized vs. decentralized strategies and I plan to expand on these concepts in my next set of essays after the release of *Get Catering and Grow Sales!* I've held this back for this conversation as it needs a larger in-depth discussion in a different venue.

You will need to make policy and procedure decisions regarding order entry specific to your own brand circumstances. A lot of these catering rules will depend on your current system structure such as *corporate* vs. *franchised* in your brand's structural mix.

Order follow-up will increase catering sales and further strengthen your customer relationships

One of the most critical tasks that you must master to help move toward catering success is your order follow-up procedure. Automated surveys should become part of your daily practices, and each and every order should be followed up by a phone call with the objective of making sure that you have done everything in your power to ensure that the customer was happy with your service.

I learned early on at Tony's Deli that most guests, when dissatisfied with their catering order would not take the time to let us know. If you do not solicit feedback and are not informed then you leave the fate of your brand experience in the hands of your guests. To protect your brand you have to take on the responsibility of serving your customers at every potential touch point in the ordering cycle. It is your responsibility to ask, listen and set right any issues that might be outstanding specific to their order.

In order to execute catering in the long run, you must get feedback to provide the details inside your operation on what is working and not working for your clients as it relates to catering.

As part of the catering service process, you must be very diligent with order follow up. This will also set you apart from your competition. Your brand will be well protected by great service and even if your product experience fails to be up to par on a particular occasion, your service levels will be so high that your clients will not only be forgiving, but they will tell their colleagues, friends and families how well you did to make the situation right for them.

Asking for more business will get you more business!

This simple strategy is one of the most effective ways of communicating to your clients that you are hungry for more of their business.

On each follow-up call, when positive feedback has been provided, your organization must be trained properly to ask for more of their business. If handled precisely, this is extremely effective for driving more sales.

In addition to asking for more business, find out if anyone else in their department or organization has a need for your catering services, and if they do, begin the selling process to that new target client by asking for a their name, address, email and phone number. When you call this new lead, you can suggest to them that their friend wanted you to send them a gift. The gift of course is your promotional catering basket. And so the selling cycle begins with this new relationship.

Providing a predictable, reliable and scalable service experience to your customers in this way will grow your catering revenues rapidly, assuming you are clear about expectations.

Production efficiency will grow your sales!

Now that we have reviewed the idea of selling these services and taking orders, we can move to a short discussion on the manufacturing and distribution process of these orders. The next link in the order cycle is order fulfillment at the store level.

The production methodology of your catering operation is a key discussion topic as it directly relates to the success of the order and can create new dynamics in your stores – and potentially many complications. Depending on your dayparts for catering, your start and stop times will be very different for catering than your in-store dayparts.

The creation of menu components for catering needs careful thought, and from a manufacturing and packaging perspective the entire process must be blueprinted and standardized. Our industry is accustomed to fulfilling orders at the POS level and for catering this simply does not work when you scale revenues. To really crank up catering sales you need to have more of a manufacturing perspective.

Planning and flexibility in your production methodology becomes an important part of this equation. In addition to this layer, you must be prepared to handle the dynamics of last-minute order adjustments, and your policies and procedures need to be well documented and executed to ensure a smooth service experience for your guests.

Let's discuss the internal timing of catering for lunch as it relates to production. Your internal preparation and order assembly will begin earlier in the day than your in-store made-to-order retail lunch. (Certainly preparation for your retail rush will be happening in parallel to the catering production and assembly). However, from early in the morning you will be manufacturing all of your catering orders and getting organized for distribution.

Depending on your menu, cold food and hot food will be handled differently for catering than it will for in-store. If implemented successfully, all your lunchtime catering orders will be on the trucks or in the coolers or hot pans by 10:45 am -11:15 am each day.

The synergy of this is the efficiency. Just as your catering lunch execution is ramping down from an internal production perspective, your retail lunch execution is about to ramp up.

This is a critical internal characteristic that you must understand in order to appreciate the magic that can take place between your catering and retail channel. Essentially, what you have achieved here using this logic, is that you have generated incremental revenue using your existing assets thereby improving and increasing your output.

Please take note: as you arrive at a more clear vision of your catering channel and you begin to clearly define your menu, policies and procedures, you will begin to raise the bar for yourself and your clients. This in turn will force you to get better and will result in more brand loyalty from your customers. But because you will now be growing more revenues out of your existing facilities with different services, there will be a point and time that you will begin to see a competition for internal resources at the store level.

This will have to be managed properly, and a plan needs to be put in place to help manage this unique dynamic. It will be an exciting time for your brand, but it needs to be thoughtfully planned out, supervised and understood.

Internal planning – for tomorrow's catering orders

Another key element in the preparation process for your catering orders is that you must start considering your plan for executing tomorrow's orders. There are so many details that need to get tended to and at Tony's Deli we used to have a single catering supervisor at each shift. Their sole responsibility on the afternoon/evening shift was to fold boxes, organize labels, prepare beverages and prepare paper service. Anything that can be done the night before, using already existing resources that might be idle in between your dayparts, is another part of the efficiency equation and contributes to the whole justification of why catering makes good business sense.

More sales equals more work however because the execution for these service channels takes place on different timing cycles, you can make better use of your in-store people. Saying that, you will have to change their job descriptions and invest in retraining them so that you set them up for success.

Catering is a high margin business.

Menu development will shift consumer behavior and drive more sales!

This is probably the single biggest challenge to overcome as an operator next to the strategic plan. It's all in your mind, and there are some physical constraints, however, when you really do the math you will understand the reasons why you need to dig in and focus on your re-invention as it relates to catering. You have worked so hard to build up your current manufacturing process for your retail operation that the very idea of layering a different menu and manufacturing process can seem daunting. I never said it was going to be easy, and I did say that it would take a strategic level commitment.

As stated earlier, catering may never be your core business however it should be part of your core strategic plan as an opportunity to get more sales. Although catering will represent a profitable and worthwhile revenue stream, it will only be thrilling because it is complementary to your existing operations. Moreover, there are few barriers to entry due to simply using your existing infrastructure. There is no big capital expenditure here as compared to building out a whole new facility.

So you need a catering menu-development program that is also very simple for your brand. Your catering menu can be packaged differently and can offer different products. Portion sizes can differ and should be constrained to the type of packaging that you decide to use in your menu development process.

I would like to see you get out of the box on this one. Every ingredient you need to build a successful catering channel currently exists in every cooler and freezer and dry goods storage area in all of your stores.

The catering menu development process is the opportunity to take your ingredient and flavor profile and develop new products that are right for your brand. Catering can be a subset experience of the current overall experience of your brand.

Once you get to this understanding, you will be able to add a parallel process for your catering program and your retail program. You will eventually manage your entire LTO (Limited Time Offer) program with catering included in the process.

I believe it's about leveraging the power of your brand across another service and consumption experience that provides a positive experience to your guests. You are simply taking your brand, and filling the demand that already exists in this market.

If as a brand you have in excess of 100 stores, you should engage a menu development expert to set up an easily executable catering menu, using your existing flavor profile. Let's use what you have first, make it simple and scalable and drive sales. Once you begin to level your catering sales curve out, you can then begin switching it up when you know you need to. I believe the market will tell you through the R&D process, and through test markets, for example. It's in your customers' best interest that you protect your brand through the experience of catering.

This tends to be today's biggest stumbling block to the world's biggest brands, as it relates to seriously considering how to execute this catering opportunity. We need to get our minds wrapped around the idea that catering is an entrepreneurial experience for our brands at this point in our industry cycle. If we look back in history, we can see entrepreneurial shifts throughout our industry that then became standard procedure for all operators.

Once we appreciate that catering is just another one of these shifts in our industry, and if we decide to proceed with our full commitment, I believe this multi-unit restaurant community will see profitability that we may never have seen before. I am certain, that the market will not only grow, but multi-unit restaurant operators will become specialists in the types of catering that we are discussing.

Let's think a little bigger here. I am certain that the model we are discussing in *Get Catering and Grow Sales!* also works perfectly for the multi-unit grocery segment. Just walk into any of their delis. I am passionate about our urgency here as a community because if we establish our community as leaders in this segment, we will have a higher probability of competing successfully in the long term as the market forces change. The grocery business will move slower, but will eventually fall into this model for their delis and in-store bakeries as well. So, we have an opportunity to jump in front and take a lead position now.

The right packaging is critical to growing sales!

Once you have conquered the flavor profile of your catering menu and you have performed the proper analysis for how your brand fits in the marketplace, your packaging and presentation will become critical towards the successful execution of the overall experience. Your packaging and presentation decisions will be critical to the consumption experience for your guests as well as dictate your food safety and handling procedures.

In my mind, the platter business is by far the easiest menu format to execute for catering. In addition, large bowls of salads that accompany your platters can round out your offerings.

At Tony's Deli, we tried everything from wicker baskets to those awful industry standard black plastic trays in the early days. Although we were able to create a platter-based menu with the trays, the packaging did not do our products justice. And they were really expensive!

One day, we decided to design our own custom corrugated box for our catering presentation and delivery, in two sizes. In addition, we had the boxes manufactured with wax linings so that we could rely on them to stay dry, should our fruit platters or antipasto platters release moisture from the time it was packaged to the time it was consumed. The wax lining allowed us to use our platters for wet and dry items, although we never mixed the two together of course.

The beautiful thing about this packaging was that not only did we brand the Tony's Deli catering experience with our look, but the boxes were elegant enough and sturdy enough that they became unique brand ambassadors in our marketplace. Because we made them so well, often they could be seen lying around the offices for months afterwards and our clients used them for sorting trays.

In addition, we got two other great benefits by using this packaging:

- The per unit cost of each tray, in comparison to the black trays that we were already using, was cheaper by more than 50 per cent. Not only did we look better on the boardroom table and improve our customer experience, we were saving money at the same time!

- The trays made for a great visual impact at the deli. As the trays arrived flat, in bundles of 25, a lot of our time went into folding them together. Once they were built, the empty ones fit perfectly into one another, and we could stack them high in the back of the deli, against the wall on a shelf. The tray stacks were noticeable and contributed to the ambience of the place. It clearly showed our guests that we were in the catering and delivery business in a big way. Those were the same platters we used every day for our deliveries.

Trays and platters – the cornerstone of a solid catering business

It is critical to always keep in mind that the catering/delivery business is about feeding groups of people, on time with accuracy.

I see operators who try to execute catering with their typical take-out packaging, which is designed for individual consumers. It doesn't work on any level for catering execution. In addition, it's inefficient in terms of space and looks terrible on the table. With platters you can be extremely creative.

For example, you might provide three sizes: small, medium and large. You can suggest that one platter size say medium, feeds from 10 to 15 people. If you price it well, you will always get the benefit of the higher guest count.

If your medium platter feeds 10 to 15 people and is $69.95, then if your client has 12 people to feed you can still recommend the same platter. Your price is still $69.95 and your manufacturing process is precise. You will have tighter control over your costs, and create a unique and predictable experience for all touch points in the order execution. Selling by the platter will make it easier for you and your customer.

Continuing with this example, if your client has 18 people, you can suggest a medium platter for $69.95 and a small platter that feeds six to 10 people for $39.95. If you include packaging with the order for handling leftovers as part of your scripted service experience anything that is left over can be taken home or distributed among the staff in the office.

Another key success factor in providing a great catering experience is to make sure that you recommend the right amount of food for fulfilling your clients' feeding requirements. You don't want to oversell your customers, but even worse than that, you don't want to undersell your customers. One of the most embarrassing things a client can experience with a catering order is that there is not enough food for the group.

At Tony's Deli we packaged as many platters as we could. We then complemented these platters with large bowls of salads and used the same size platters to provide desserts and fruit. We had an upscale version using our platters for fruit presentations, cheese presentations, vegetable platters, antipasto platters and so on.

For our hors d'oeuvres experience in the evening we sold all our menu items by the dozen. And once produced, we used these same custom trays to present and deliver them to our customers.

Box lunches – focus on volume

If box lunches are produced in large batches and there is ample space to do so then there is an opportunity to sell them in volumes. Tours, schools and large seminar gatherings are perfect markets for box lunches.

Keep in mind that box-lunch manufacturing and assembly are time-intensive activities. If you are going to offer a box lunch on your menus, I recommend that you think big. Ask for a minimum of 100 box lunches to fill an order. Then it will be worth your time and energy to tool up the assembly that is required for these box products.

From my experience as an operator, the only way a successful box lunch program works, is if you can really crank out the volume. Anything less than that tends to get very cumbersome for the kitchen and the manufacturing process will compete with the more efficient process of trays and platters.

Beverages – think about creating a proprietary beverage

Selling beverages to the catering market is part of the up-selling process. Saying that, there are certain beverages in the marketplace that are very price sensitive such as soft drinks, juices and bottled water. Most people know what the price of a can of coke is sold at in the grocery segment.

To overcome this price sensitivity, I recommend that each of you have a lower-end, medium-end and higher-end beverage program. In addition, I recommend that you create a proprietary beverage such as Iced Tea or Lemonade and sell it by the gallon. This will allow you to increase your opportunity for creating a crave-able proprietary beverage experience, which in itself can potentially draw customers and yield higher margins. The idea of a signature beverage will work very well here, so if you are known for your homemade iced tea, this is a great venue to move some product.

Beverages should be chilled the night before, and the catering lead person on the shift should make sure all the beverages are bagged or boxed and organized for the next day's distribution.

Another great idea as it relates to catering beverages is to limit the number of beverage selections. You can charge for extras here such as bags of ice, if you are set up to provide these value-added items.

Hot food vs. cold food

Hot food is typically more difficult to execute for a catering delivery program. If you offer hot food, then you should try to offer a limited menu selection. A good pasta program is fairly simple to execute, for example. Mexican fare can also be manageable, however, it is critical to source the right packaging in order to ensure a high quality experience. I have seen many fajita bars and/or taco bars executed flawlessly for catering.

In order to do hot food well for catering, your packaging program will have to be particularly well thought out. Temperature controls will have to be in place and your execution timing and delivery will be more difficult.

Hot items such as soups, pasta and fajita bars, can be offered, but for the corporate delivery business I recommend staying with a cold program if you are a beginner. I appreciate that for some brands this might prove to be difficult, however, I want to encourage you to think about the idea of leveraging your brand across new products. Keeping it simple is the key.

Your strongest corporate catering dayparts will be breakfast and lunch. There is a plethora of menu choices that you can provide for those dayparts where the food is fresh and fast, and unheated. More importantly, no chafing dishes are required for a cold-catering program.

As an example, a continental breakfast with fresh squeezed orange juice will work for breakfast. Of course, you'll have to get the coffee there hot, but there are a lot of disposable containers as well as more equipment available for doing this job well. At Tony's Deli we used to lean on our coffee vendor to supply us with all the equipment we needed to execute a strong morning catering program.

Look at a lox and cream cheese platter for the main protein in the meal, and of course don't forget the fresh fruit for breakfast.

As far as corporate catering execution is concerned, most operators will find it easier to execute a cold catering menu.

I know operators whose core business is hamburgers, and helping them to get their minds wrapped around a cold-based catering program does not come easily.

I would like to point out here again that the main objective of entering this marketplace is to leverage your brands across this channel. My advice to the "hamburger brands" is to get away from the grill and develop a sandwich and salad program that will travel well and will still keep your brand experience within your flavor profile. I am sure this will be a great debate in the years ahead.

As we go down this path together, it is important that you each take the lead to follow all of the necessary food handling and safety procedures. Refrigeration planning is, therefore, a very important part of your overall catering execution.

As you consider your delivery options, you'll want to make sure that temperature controls are in place from the onset. If you are able to execute properly on holding times, you will be in a great position to use that as a selling feature to your customers. Food safety is a very important part of the overall experience, and is a key selling feature that your organization can use for keeping client confidence.

To be done well, you need to make sure that it is publicized and that you celebrate the fact that you take special care to ensure that your menu items are safely prepared and transported to ensure that your food is being consumed at the right temperature.

If your concept is mainly built around hot food at the retail level, do not fret. As I have mentioned time and time again, the idea here is to simply leverage the power of your brand across a new sales channel. As such, your catering products can, and should be different than those menu items you sell in your stores.

Manufacturing efficiency will help to grow sales!

As discussed so often in this book, catering is a different business. In order to execute any sort of volume in this business channel, you must understand that in fact you are a manufacturer. The typical order dynamic for catering is that you will have some advance notice, however, it is dynamic and changing as you approach the preparation and distribution of the orders for the day.

You need to look at your production efficiency to make the catering business work well for your environment. Production needs to be looked at from an overall daily production level, as opposed to a made-to-order type of experience, such as an in-store process.

There are many gains to be made when executing bulk-catering orders. Your ability for planning will be important in terms of your overall order execution.

You should look at your menu items, and make sure that you are prepared to portion them in bulk so that the catering experience comes off properly.

For the most part, the preparation part of your day for catering should happen the day before, with a view to being flexible for last-minute orders and order adjustments. To help with the latter, you should have some good solid policies and procedures in place so that you can focus on providing a predictable service experience to your guests. Sometimes saying "no" to your guests is not only in their best interest but also in the best interest of your brand.

Do you have visibility into your catering operations?

Planning the catering production process properly will create more capacity for growing sales!

Before your kitchen closes for the day, the next day's catering raw material production should be portioned, sliced and diced. Shelf stable items such as paper service, beverages and chips can be gathered and prepared for the next day's shipping.

Once your raw materials are portioned for your fresh production for the next day, these assembly items should be well marked and date rotated to ensure fresh end products for your customers and easy assembly for your morning production crew.

In the morning on the day of your catering execution, all fresh items that need to be baked or are brought in from third-party vendors need to be on site much earlier than the typical items for your retail operations.

If you plan properly, your early morning production crew should be able to focus all of their attention on the assembly of the menu items and the orders. When your volume increases it will come down to managing an assembly line by menu item, and then each of those items can be moved into a space where you can now package the orders up according to your packing slips on a per-order basis.

Production time is really "assembly time"!

As discussed above, pre-production should happen as late in the day as possible the previous day. If you have planned well, on the day of catering production and distribution, most of the kitchen's energy should go into assembly and packaging of orders.

Once orders are all out for the day, then preparation for tomorrow's catering should begin. Slicing, dicing and chopping. Making sure all of the portions are measured for the next day's catering assembly. And so the cycle continues.

I will point out again that I often see operators trying to fulfill catering orders on a per-order basis. I strongly discourage this practice and encourage you to think of catering as a high-volume production line. The key to success here is to focus well on the pre-production process and if you have planned and prepared well, then on the day of order fulfillment you will be more effective at your flow through.

Solid vendor management can grow sales!

Depending on your specific environment, enrolling your vendors in your catering operation will become very important in terms of your end goal of growing catering sales. Each of your vendors need to understand that catering is a core business strategy for your brand, and they must appreciate that in order for you to execute properly for your guests, their services and actions may have to change, as well, based on the workflow required to fill the demand for your catering services.

For example, raw material deliveries may have to arrive earlier or later on any given day than previously agreed to. If you have a big catering day the next day, your vendors need to be flexible and be able to deliver additional raw materials on short notice. Hopefully, once you become more proficient and consistent in your sales you will be better at inventory planning. Your vendors will need to work hard with you to be able to help grow sales in this segment.

If your vendors do not understand the subtleties of issues such as last-minute order swells and order adjustments, then they will have a difficult time reacting to your needs as your catering revenues grow.

You must manage your raw material vendors appropriately and enforce your vendor policies and procedures around the needs of this channel. After all, more sales for you translates to more sales for them as well.

Using your existing labor more effectively will increase your overall unit level margins!

Discussion on this topic is difficult for many operators to integrate. The difficulty here is that because catering revenues are layered on top of your already existing operations, the functional areas between retail and catering can become grey and muddled. As a manager, you need to have a clear definition for your labor force and as your catering sales grow, they will begin to compete for resources internally at the unit level. In my experience, I view this as one of the biggest challenges facing our community. Your people need to be invested in your catering channel and you must re-engineer their roles and responsibilities if you are to make room for catering in your current environment.

When you begin your catering program it will become very important to create all of the defined roles at the unit level. You must expect that some of your existing labor resources will become shared by both your retail and catering execution. Saying that, it is critical that you re-train your people in the right tasks. At the unit level, if you can use your existing labor to help facilitate the production and assembly of catering orders you will yield higher overall unit sales and drive down your per unit labor costs. This will result in an increase of your overall operating unit margin.

As discussed, preparation for catering begins during the last shift of the previous day. There should be a catering-lead person left for preparation in the kitchen to make sure that all is in order for the following day's catering production and assembly. Your front-counter labor resources should be engaged with preparing beverages as well as paper service and/or folding boxes and other catering related activities that will speed up tomorrow's production and assembly. You must work as a team.

An operational adjustment that you will need to consider here is that on the morning of your catering execution, you will require an earlier start to the day in the kitchen. These catering-lead people will ensure that your catering day is set up for success.

If you have a morning segment for your retail business, your early morning crew will be well into the production of catering by the time you open the doors of your stores. Remember, breakfast orders need to be on the trucks or ready for pick-up by 6:30 am or 7:00 am, and all your lunch orders for delivery and pick-up need to be on the trucks and ready to roll by 11:15 am to be able to get the food delivered on time.

This results in a very dynamic environment however, the execution can get a bit hairy on any given day as you will also be executing on your retail operations in between these times.

A major point here, as it relates to leveraging your labor pool, is that instead of hiring for new positions, you can simply add in some "catering-related tasks" to your existing labor pool. From there, you may have to insert one or two key catering lead people for proper execution, but you would only do that as your sales are growing.

You will live or die by your order execution!

You are only going to grow this revenue channel if your order execution and fulfillment are exceptional. You must remember that anything less than that will dilute your brand and provide a negative experience to your customers.

You must focus your resources on getting the orders right, and there are many critical factors that come into play here for your team to be successful in this channel. As you have now learned, the execution dynamics of this channel are different than those of your existing retail channels and once your orders leave the front door, because you no longer have your products and services within your four walls, the risk of failure goes up. You must do everything you can to mitigate that risk.

Operations manuals have to be in place, your training and communication has to be impeccable, and your accuracy and quality have to be in line with the expectation of your brand, your organization and your customers.

If you fail at the execution level, you will not succeed in growing this business stream.

Do you want your catering deliveries **to be** on time, **every time?**

Preparing for distribution properly will be critical to your customers' experience!

On the day of your order execution, distributing the orders on time is one of the most complex considerations that you need to think about.

One key role in the catering execution chain is your delivery coordinator. This individual is responsible for mapping out the deliveries the day before, as well as making sure that the trucks are gassed up and safe to drive. There is nothing worse than loading up a truck with deliveries only to find out that the truck does not start. There should be a truck safety check at the end of each shift.

The delivery coordinator will work from their delivery log for the day. They will assign orders to drivers and organize someone internally to help with catering pick-up orders.

In addition, they will coordinate the orders off the production line and generate all the labels for the orders.

They may also coordinate a third-party delivery service as well. The main message that I'd like to leave you with here is that before distribution of the orders can happen, they need to be organized and prepared properly. Pack slips need to be checked off and each driver must have all their instructions and invoices prior to leaving for their destinations.

Distribution methodologies are a strategic and managerial preference

The last step in the execution process prior to consumption is that the orders arrive at their destinations, to the guests who were intended to have your brand experience.

There are various distribution models for our multi-unit restaurant environments, but for the most part the key decision you need to make is whether you want to outsource deliveries, manage deliveries internally, or do both.

In some downtown urban markets I have seen order walkers, for example in San Francisco, Chicago and New York. These "order-walkers" take orders to their delivery targets on foot with branded carts.

Of course, the easiest method of distribution is a pick-up catering order. You should definitely set up a dedicated space in your stores that is clearly marked "catering pick-up" which could be next to but separate from the "take-out pick-up" counters. I would encourage you to make sure that you keep true to separating out the process of your "pickup orders for take-out" versus your "pickup orders for catering". Each customer needs to be handled differently and methodically when they show up at your counter for the channel from which they have ordered.

Should you manage drivers internally or contract third-party drivers? The big debate!

This part of our conversation can be debated for hours. On the one hand, your own drivers have all of the liabilities that go along with being employees. In your catering-driven market, volume might warrant some of your own drivers. At the same time, these employee drivers can help manage any third-party drivers that can help with distribution overflow on very busy catering days.

I have seen different compensation models, from hourly plus mileage to just hourly as well as a flat fee per delivery, which in some cases can get passed on to your customers.

You will have idle labor in your current environment. Perhaps, some of that idle labor can be allocated to doing what they can do to get the deliveries out the door.

At Tony's Deli, I engaged both my own drivers and third-party delivery drivers. It worked pretty well. We even worked with several courier companies, though if you do look down the courier path, make sure you train them to know the way you want your orders dropped off.

As we have discussed, the distribution point for your catering orders is the high-risk point for your catering execution. Many things can go wrong once your orders leave your four walls and it is imperative that you understand how to mitigate these risks.

Saying "please" and "thank you" at the delivery point can help grow catering sales!

Displaying good manners should be part of the brand experience. Delivery staff should always say "please" and "thank you" when dropping off orders. They need to ask if there is more that they can do for the customer. They should always carry extra beverages on the trucks and extra paper service. (But make sure you charge for them!). In addition, you must make sure that you enroll your drivers to double check that the customer is ok before leaving as well as teach them to ask for referrals and for more business.

Of course, any information that the driver picks up regarding additional services should be passed on to the right sales coordinator for a follow up call.

Some key responsibilities for your primary drivers

- Keep trucks clean and maintained and always in a "ready" position.

- Check driver log today, for the next day and keep all paperwork organized for deliveries.

- Upon reporting for work, the primary driver's main function is to take the orders that have been assembled and packaged by the kitchen, sort them out for their routes, and pass on directions to other delivery drivers.

- Report all delivery problems back to the primary driver who makes sure that the customer gets the right follow-up.

- These functions should take up only four hours of a person's day. The other part of their shift should be spent on "jumping in" where necessary to help get all the orders out the door.

A few thoughts regarding outsourcing drivers

I will just touch on this briefly again here. Third-party drivers can be a good strategy for certain stores where catering might only do $500 per day. You will also have stores that might do $2,000 per day. It will depend largely on location and the strength of the demand for catering in that market – the busier stores should have their own drivers.

The liability factor can be a big reason to outsource as well. As contractors, they take on more risk, which can be a good thing. However, saying that, be prepared to give up on margin, because you have to pay them more per delivery in order for them to economically run their own trucks and cover ongoing running and maintenance costs such as insurance, fuel and general vehicle maintenance.

As you go down this path, you must keep in mind that the market will only bear so much for a delivery charge.

Catering finance and accounting is customer service work and will have a positive impact on growing sales!

Accounts Receivables

My focus in *Get Catering and Grow Sales!* has been on the corporate catering segment. As you have learned by now, this requires you to think about your brand as it relates to a business-to-business selling strategy and a different market structure. By the very nature of what it is, your financial relationship in this segment will be with corporations. When it comes to selling to corporations, making provisions for a credit facility is not only expected but it is also standard operating procedure in the business world. As a food retailer, this type of thinking naturally goes against the grain.

In my experience, allowing for house accounts not only keeps customers coming back for more business, it also builds more trust between your customer and your brand. If leveraged properly providing credit to your regular customers will keep them coming back more often because you not only make it easy on them but you also tell them how much you trust them. This builds a lot of goodwill in your business relationships that will serve you in the long run. By extending credit, you have more reasons to call them for more business! Even the collection process provides a selling opportunity if handled properly.

I recognize that this is a BIG paradigm shift because we, as a community, are so accustomed to operating in a cash based environment. I acknowledge here that all of our raw materials are consumed at the point of delivery and our labor is paid every two weeks. In addition, our vendors try to get paid in Net 7 or 15 days if they can. (Of course this is different for each of us depending on our purchasing power). As such, many of you find it difficult to add in the dynamic and costs of managing receivables into your businesses.

I have thought long and hard about this issue and have concluded that by not allowing your corporate customers to set up house accounts for the gift of giving you their business on a regular basis, you are in fact communicating that you don't want to do business. In the business world credit is used and given on many transactions every single day. That is how business is done when trading corporation to corporation.

I have no doubt that there are many CFOs out there that will disagree with the idea of providing credit facilities to corporations and I'd welcome the debate. I am a firm believer that cash is king, but I also believe that sales solve most business problems. And hence a balance must be struck.

The right billing system will help grow sales!

In order for your organization to be able to sell your catering services, you will need to have a catering billing system that is dedicated specifically to running all of your catering transactions. It must allow you to set up and manage corporate accounts, generate invoices and apply payments against those invoices. In addition, you will need to be able to provide your catering customers with account activity statements.

Of course, you will need enforced policies and procedures and strong leadership in place to manage payment collections, but there are many efficient ways to deal with that. If working on a larger scale, you can even engage a third-party agency to collect money once your business has grown to the point where it can make sense. For now, let's assume this is an internal function of your catering operation's bookkeeping department.

We'll discuss centralization strategies in the discussion series #17 that will follow this manuscript. You will find a list of all the discussion topics in the appendix to follow. The accounting and cash cycle needs to be well understood to help move you towards gaining overall control over this rate-limiting factor for growing your catering sales to their full potential.

As mentioned, House Accounts will make it a lot of easier for your clients to spend more money with you. You'll just have to get very good at managing it.

Why using existing POS assets for catering transactions is dangerous for your brand

Many in our community that I speak with make the strategic error of believing their existing POS systems can be the transaction engine for catering in their operations. I am clear that POS systems are not geared to handle the subtleties of our catering transactions and that they do not have the right business logic to handle the intricacies of what we need as a community to service and grow this channel properly. Catering is a different business and requires its own set of tools if we are to seriously consider growing sales as a community.

Since catering orders are often taken by telephone, conversational ordering systems that can be used during the order entry process with the customer are required, so that you may provide them with a consistent and predictable service experience. To do so, you must control your business well and follow a fixed and predictable script as it pertains to the execution of your orders.

From the beginning you need an order-entry system to generate invoices, statements, collection notices and so on. It will be necessary to adjust your mindset about what cash flow looks like in the catering business. Naturally the system will also extend into the production and distribution process.

Your system of choice for catering transactions should be web based so that customers can also place orders online. These order entry systems will also need to encompass the selling process, production process and distribution process of all the catering orders.

These "catering systems" as I will refer to them should then feed the appropriate "catering data" to your above store systems. Some examples of possible integration points might be directly to your food cost system, accounting systems and your business intelligence systems. With the right catering software and technology service provider you will be able to drive the catering data through the data path that you need it to go through so that it feeds into your existing technology infrastructure and your existing reporting architectures.

Items on your catering menu can be priced higher than on your retail menu.

Pricing strategy

In order to provide a positive service experience for your guests, as it relates to catering, you must become an expert in this business. Since you will become an expert in catering, the price you select to sell at should be commensurate with the service and experience level, as it relates to the overall pricing strategy of your brand.

In order to resource the right assets to provide that experience, you will need to make sure that you completely understand your catering margins.

I would like to speak to the internal decision that you need to make between your in-store menu, prices and portions vs. your catering/delivery menu, prices and portions.

From what I have learned, you **DO NOT** have to charge equally in the catering revenue channel, just as you do not have to sell the same menu items. As an operator, you can make new creations for your catering guests, items that are LTO (Limited Time Offer) for catering.

As a brand parent, to position yourself well in this market, I would recommend that you begin by providing a more "upscale, healthier" version of your existing menu, at the same time preserving your brand. For example, if I were a leading a big international chicken chain, I might create a Chicken Caesar Salad that feeds 8 to 10 people, another size that feeds 12 to 18 people and so on.

It is difficult for me to comment on what the overall pricing strategies should be for the catering segment, compared to the market that needs to be discussed, however, the lesson here is that when comparing your retail prices to your catering prices, you should not hold back on making catering a great value-added experience for your guests. If you pull it off right your customers will pay a small premium for that high value experience. At the same time you will have made sure you have covered your explicit costs as well as the implicit costs that can be difficult to quantify in catering.

Management and metrics

Like every business, there are simple metrics that should be measured and celebrated in your organization as they relate to the catering revenue channel. Please note that this is not an exhaustive list and that there might be hundreds of metrics that you need to measure at all touch points of the transaction experience.

Here are some of my own:

Sales - Depending on your menu mix, your average catering order will be between $125 and $200. I have no hard data to support this, so please know that the caveat here is that this is just my experience. Based on five orders per day, that translates to $625 to $1,000 per day, in incremental revenue for each one of your locations that can perform at this level. Primarily, catering as defined here will be a five-day per week business, although you may get surprised on the odd Saturday. So, weekly revenues at the unit level could be increased from $3,125 to $5,000 per week, per store. If you have 100 stores, then you are discussing $312,500 to $500,000 per week in incremental sales across your existing infrastructure. Extend that potential to the length of a year, and you have a channel that can be anywhere from $14.9 million to $24.0 million for your brand. If you can add one more order per day, then you are really singing the praise. I have calculated this number based on a 48-week annual opportunity. This takes into account holiday shutdowns.

I have approached this conservatively as I am not considering Saturdays or Sundays as potential catering revenue days.

Some additional metrics to consider tracking

Sleepy clients - One of the key metrics you look at in the catering business is frequency of order. Remember, in catering you are trying to get your brand experience on your clients' corporate catering rotation list. You must look at your database of clients that have not ordered from you in the last 60 to 90 days. This needs to be measured if you are to grow your catering revenues with any consistency. You must understand why your customer is no longer ordering from you and you must get into the practice of asking the right questions to find out why their order patterns might have changed.

Menu mix - You must consistently look at your menu mix. You will begin to see patterns where 80 percent of your catering revenue is coming from 20 percent of your menu items. As you interpret this data, you need to use it to modify your pricing and eliminate products that are not selling. By optimizing your menu mix, you will make catering easier on your operations.

Service performance reports - As part of the overall customer experience, follow up calls should be made diligently and wholeheartedly. Your customer service representatives should listen to what your clients are saying and then take the time to write it up. If it is a complaint, then you must make sure it is escalated properly internally to make it right for your customers. If you provide that type of timely, accurate service to your catering clients, they will buy from you consistently because they trust you to look after their needs properly.

Lead conversion reports - In order to build your catering sales, your organization will need to engage in active selling, business to business. Part of the selling process will be to target leads that work in organizations in your community and make the effort to pursue a business relationship with them. If you are investing resources into that effort, it is important to understand how long it takes to convert a lead to a client as well as how much time passes between your initial prospecting and when they migrate to a customer. Keep in mind here again that the relationship will go with the client wherever they go and not with the account.

How to make a profit with catering

Below is a list of some key items to consider. It is in no particular order of importance:

- Keep your eye on the ball when it comes to catering. It is a completely different business than the business of retail. For this reason, approach it with respect. Get your business strategy in order first.

- Remember that the key academic element for profits from this channel is that you are launching an alternative service experience to your existing customers, thereby servicing another need for your customers from your existing infrastructure where it makes sense to do so.

- Use brand leverage to launch your catering services. Leverage the goodwill you have in your existing markets. Use every customer touch point as an opportunity to explain these services and make it easy for your customers to inquire.

- Develop your catering menu first. For those of us with more complex infrastructures to manage, make sure this menu is kept simple. You can use your existing flavor profile and invest well in your messaging and packaging. As time passes, you must invest in catering menu R&D processes to keep the program fresh and exciting for your customers.

- Invest in creating a formal catering structure internally with the right leadership to drive this part of your business. In turn, provide a vision of catering for your organization. Make it part of your core business strategy.

- Create a policy and procedure manual for corporate and franchised stores.

- Invest in training your people in the language of catering and provide them with direction of how to handle your customers when they visit.

- Invest in outbound selling, business to business.

- Invest in the right systems and technology for ease of ordering and flawless execution.

- Provide stellar customer service for catering through all aspects of your customer touch points.

- Follow up diligently.

- Provide a higher and fresher quality experience for your guests at the point of consumption. Ensure that your products travel well to their destinations. Remove items that do not.

- Define metrics for improvement and measure against them. What you measure will improve.

Of course, there are many other elements that I could list here, however, I believe that these are some key high-level items that we need to put in place to be able to take the next steps together.

Catering is not about

online ordering.

The right technology and software will grow sales!

There are several items to discuss as they relate to how catering software fits into the existing IT infrastructure.

My intention in writing this manuscript has been to provide our community with essential information to make the catering stream work well for every operator. Saying that, there is a point in time where you will each reach a scale in your revenues where software and IT will play a critical role to keeping your catering business organized and streamlined.

Committing to the right catering software system

One of the biggest lessons I learned early on in my career was that you were only as good as your manual systems, never your software systems. In the early days, there were no computers and so systems were developed manually long before they were developed as software. And so, I want to point out emphatically that it is less about software and more about the business logic you apply to managing your business.

How will you know when the right software system comes along for your catering business? I will suggest here that the right software system will be obvious once you make a commitment to becoming a domain expert in catering. The reason for this has everything to do with using the intellectual property of other experts who understand it and have developed software around the right business logic that is required to grow and maintain a profitable catering business in a multi-unit restaurant environment.

It is critical, from a usability perspective, that the correct data is gathered from the client at the point of order capture. The right software system will provide you that transparency. In addition, once fully deployed, your catering system should be fully integrated with your back-end reporting systems such as food cost systems, accounting systems and POS systems, where it makes sense.

Any catering software platform that you consider should be web-based in today's world. The platform selected should be an enterprise-based system and the database should be standardized, to easily help share data across all functional areas of your organization. Your selected catering software should be able to communicate with all modern-day technologies.

Is POS integration required for catering sales?

There is a big discussion to be had around this topic. Most of the market believes that POS integration for catering is a requirement. In my experience, POS integration *is not required for the catering transaction.*

Today's point-of-sale systems are not built with the right business logic that is required to succeed in the catering market. So, if you are suggesting that you need POS integration for catering orders for executing those orders, I will defend defiantly that POS integration for the purpose of catering order execution is a strategic error for your catering operations as it is the wrong tool. Using this strategy will not allow you to scale the production and distribution that catering will demand.

If you simply need to dump the data into the POS system as part of an automated day-end procedure as you poll your store data, then I am the first to agree with this strategy, as it relates to catering. Although you do not need to rely on your POS infrastructure to handle your catering transactions, you may need to integrate your catering software into your POS infrastructure for the simple task of gathering end of day data. This decision will largely depend on your data flow structure that you have in place today.

But there are instances, for catering transactions, where data can be injected into above store systems, and as such the POS system is not required at all.

If an additional objective is to find solutions for online ordering for take-out, then integration into your POS system via the web certainly makes sense for that transaction type.

But that again, is another revenue stream for your brand to consider. Do not get confused between online ordering and catering software. They are very different animals and serve completely different purposes.

Stop, slow down and take the time to make the right decisions for your catering strategy.

Conclusion – what's the right strategy for your organization?

If you are a multi-unit restaurant operator, and have established infrastructure, then the right strategy for your brand is to develop and commit to a catering strategy.

Even if that strategy is to not to go into the catering segment, then be happy with your decision, but make a deliberate decision about taking this path. One of my personal goals of writing *Get Catering and Grow Sales!* is to create discussion to help us think about it. I want to make sure you have really taken the time to understand the impact that this revenue channel can have on your top-line sales, your overall gross margins and your bottom line at the unit level.

As demonstrated earlier, although catering may only represent 20 percent of your top line sales, the contribution to the gross dollar margin will blow your socks off. But you'll need to do it right.

There is always more to discuss but as I mentioned at the beginning, my intention was to provide a new perspective on catering in a multi-unit restaurant environment. My hope is that this book will also provide a compass for direction that our community can turn to as we begin the hard work of implementing these concepts into our operations. I am certain that in the years to come, catering will make up a substantial component of our industry revenues and we will become experts at executing this channel across our existing assets.

I plan to provide a venue for more learning through our ongoing *Catering Makes Sense Webinar Series* as we move forward. I invite each of you to contact me to discuss new ideas as well as to debate those that I have put forward here.

Over the next 12 months or so, my plan is to write nineteen additional discussion papers to expand on these topics. You will find a list of those items in the appendix to follow. Please make sure each of you sign up at www.monkeymediasoftware.com to receive them should you be interested in learning more.

Hopefully by now you can appreciate the logic of using your brand and organizational leverage to drive incremental catering sales. Furthermore, I hope you see the importance that our industry recognizes this opportunity, and puts standards in place by which we can measure ourselves. As I stated earlier, I firmly believe that the corporate catering market is under-served by our community, and every brand, in every segment, should consider what their business could look like when their catering channel has reached its potential.

Finally, I hope we all invest in this channel as a community with our ideas, innovations, resources and time. Let's share information and take ourselves seriously as "caterers" as defined in *Get Catering and Grow Sales!* If we work on this together, we will all prosper.

Appendix: Get Catering and Grow Sales!: A Discussion Series

Watch for these Essays and more in the very near future:

Discussion #1 - Our margins in our catering operations

Discussion #2 - Increasing our catering order volume and frequency

Discussion #3 - Further defining the service script

Discussion #4 - Managing order size

Discussion #5 - Understanding the implicit costs of catering

Discussion #6 - The cost of distribution

Discussion #7 - Understanding the explicit costs of catering

Discussion #8 - Streamlining operations

Discussion #9 - Planning catering production

Discussion #10 - Ensuring product quality and proper food handling

Discussion #11 - Procedures for handling the dynamics of order changes

Discussion #12 - Watch for competing resources and what to do when that happens

Discussion #13 - Marketing strategies for catering

Discussion #14 - Allocating labor to our catering operations

Discussion #15 - Managing internal "catering politics" – keeping it all on track

Discussion #16 - Compensation and bonus plans for catering

Discussion # 17 - Centralization strategies

Discussion #18 - How to perfect deliveries

Discussion #19 - Defining a catering vision and customer experience

Acknowledgements

Allow me to acknowledge my entire team at MonkeyMedia Software. If not for their daily dedication to our customers and their deep belief in the work we do, I never would have had the support at the office to actually complete *Get Catering and Grow Sales!* I am so fortunate to have an incredibly diverse group of people to work with and thank you for your trust in my vision for MonkeyMedia Software.

In alphabetical order by first name;

Alexey Voronkov, Andriy Butskiy, Benny Li, Chris Mayes, Chris Roy, Dan Ettling, Danielle Wolff, Doneen Swart, Elena Rudnitski, Giessel Razavi, Johanna Israel-Duprey, John Dumbrille, Lisa DeFeo, Lisa Jenkins, Lisa Nguyen, Marc Munro, Mark Taylor, Mike Tyler Gillies, Naomi Kawasaki, Phyo Pine, Radoslav Entchev, Ruchita Prasad, Terry Matthews, Vickie Frisbie, Vinay Jindal and Warren Neily.

A BIG acknowledgement to Mo Asgari, MonkeyMedia Software's Chief Operating Officer and Director of Technology. You have been a great and reliable partner over the last four years. Thank you for always having your iphone on your hip and for rolling up your sleeves to get the job done.

Also to our Director of Solutions Hyung Min Park, who has been there with me since the beginning of monkey history, and for his tireless hours committed to keeping our customers satisfied at all times.

In addition, there are many people who believed in me along the way. To name just a few: Peter Bonner, Mark Roberts, Dick Benmore, Jeff Lowe, Andy Mollica, Ari Weinzweig, Grace Singleton, Jeff Balin, Jim Irwin, Lindsey Schwartz, Sophia Polyak, Willy Bitter, John Clay, Steve Sarver, Clayton Chan, Lance Paine, Pat Sullivan, Molly Wilmot, Greg Cartozian, Kevin Piper, Frank Kitchens, Stuart Zaro, Trish Karter, Scott Miller, Thomas Lefort, Dan and Jeff Brunello, Bobbie Lloyd, Ricky Eisen, Pascal Rigo, Paul Barron, Dr. Tom Feltenstein, Ed Frechette, Ed Zimmerman, Jay Zimmerman, Chad Penner, Marc Halperin, Wayne Alexander, Jeff Drake, Annica Kreider, George Green, Valerie Killifer, John Livingston, William Stitt, Thomas Hadrys, Beth Briggs, Vance Carlton, and Frank Geier. Also, Frank Paci, Charles Corley, Randy White, James O'Reilly, Patrick Renna, Paul Coleman, Lesley Stowe, Maggie Arrow, Wendy Ewers, Tara Barnett, Chris Adrews, Andrew Parr, Valerie Killifer, Louis Basile, Bobby Renaud, Dick Good, Eugene Drezner and Cathryn Atkinson.

My sincere gratitude

To my parents, Rhoda and Irving Dardick, for instilling in me the value of hard work.

To my in-laws Dr. Eduardo and Gloria Schwartz, for their love and support and for always believing in me and encouraging me to further my quest for knowledge in all aspects of my life.

To H.K. for his heart and willingness to participate in my vision for MonkeyMedia Software. I am forever grateful for your kindness and generosity.

Thanks to my good friend Gord Kushner, for his never-ending support over the course of our 28-year friendship. Much of what we discussed over the years helped me when it came to finding the will to sit down and write *Get Catering and Grow Sales!*

To our loyal Monkey customers who believe in what we do and who continue to give us their trust and provide us with the opportunity to make their businesses better alongside their teams. Also, thanks to all of you for the flexibility in allowing us to make it right when it sometimes goes wrong.

To Dave Wolfgram, CEO of Forklift Brands, for really believing in our multi-unit catering model and for sharing his vision of what catering meant to his organization. Dave is a visionary and really opened his heart to allow us the opportunity to work on his businesses with him.

To Dan Dominguez of Einstein Noah Restaurant Group for calling me back after four years of leaving voice mails. Dan, that call reminds me never to give up, no matter what. I am forever grateful.

And special thanks **to you** for slowing down long enough to read *Get Catering and Grow Sales!* If you feel it was worth your time, I will consider myself very fortunate. Please forward your feedback along to getcatering@monkeymediasoftware.com

Notes

Notes

Notes

Notes

Notes

Notes

Notes